Tax Sale
Secrets Revealed

Little Known Tips and Tricks to Buy Real Estate at Tax Sales

BuyTaxSales.com

R. Sam Price
Attorney at Law

Red Carnation Homes, LLC
P.O. Box 23089
San Bernardino, CA 92406
sam@buytaxsales.com

ISBN: 978-0-9849472-0-1
ISBN: 978-0-9849472-1-8 (eBook)

This publication is designed to provide accurate and authoritative information in regard to the subject matter covered. It is sold with the understanding that the publisher is not engaged in rendering legal, accounting, or other professional services. If legal or other expert assistance is required, the services of a competent professional person should be sought.

—from the declaration of principles jointly adopted by a committee of the American Bar Association and a committee of publishers

To Mom,

You've always been there to cheerfully support everything I do.

Contents

About the Author

R. Sam Price is an attorney, real estate broker, and general contractor. He actively invests in real estate and develops residential property. He enjoys writing and teaching, especially in the field of real estate.

Sam grew up in a real estate family. His grandmother and father were both real estate brokers, and his mother was a real estate investor. He grew up surrounded by rentals and real estate deals.

Sam first entered the family business at age six by helping to hammer nails out of salvaged boards so no one would step on them. Over time, he helped with every aspect of managing rentals, buying properties, fixing properties, and selling properties.

Sam received his Bachelor of Arts degree in business administration with a concentration in finance from California State University, San Bernardino. He earned his law degree from Western New England College School of Law. He studied taxation for his master of laws degree from New York University School of Law.

After working as an international tax attorney, Sam went back into the business of real estate. Besides being a real estate investor and developer, Sam is a general contractor and a real estate broker who lists and sells properties. He also practices as an attorney.

PART I
Secrets to Finding and Researching Real Estate Bargains at Tax Sales

Chapter 1

The Basics: Introduction to Tax Sales

Chapter Overview

In this chapter, you will learn the following:

1. What are tax sale auctions?
2. What are tax lien certificates?
3. What are the benefits of tax sales?
4. The differences between tax sales and foreclosures
5. The differences between tax sales and HUD auctions

Introduction

You can purchase real estate in many ways. The most common method is to go to a real estate agent and ask to be shown properties. Another way is to approach the seller of a property directly so you don't have to pay a commission to a real estate agent. Still another way is to attend an auction of properties for sale.

A tax sale is a type of property auction held by the county. Tax sales offer a little known way to purchase real estate for a very low price. Tax sales require some legwork, but the rewards are huge.

What Are Tax Sales?

If you are reading this book, you may already have heard a bit about tax sales. The simplest explanation is that a tax sale is a real estate auction held by a county government. Anyone can buy property at a tax sale. The opening bid (minimum purchase price) of properties at a tax sale is extremely low—a fraction of the market value of the property. I've personally seen the opening bid on a piece of real estate start at $100. Where else are you going to buy a property for $100?

But how can the county sell property at such low prices? Why don't they sell for more? What is the purpose of a tax sale?

Let's first find out how the county sells property for such a low price. The background of tax sales starts with property taxes. Counties collect property taxes on real estate to generate revenue. The tax—usually between 1 to 2% of the value of the property per year—is collected twice a year. These property taxes help pay for schools, roads, services, and everything else that counties provide. Without these taxes, counties would go broke.

When a property owner does not pay his or her property taxes, the taxes go into default and become a tax lien against the real estate. After years of a property owner defaulting on the taxes, the county has the right to offer the real estate for sale to pay off the back taxes. In essence, the county forecloses on the tax lien by selling the property to collect the amount owed. To sell the real estate to pay off the back property taxes, the county holds a public auction. This public auction to foreclose on the tax lien is the county tax sale (often called the county defaulted-property tax sale).

Generally, the property is sold for the amount of property taxes owed plus the costs of the sale. This is why the property sells for only a fraction of its market value. The opening bid has nothing to do with how much the property is actually worth. The opening bid reflects the amount needed to pay the defaulted taxes that the previous owner should have paid.

The purpose of tax sales is to keep money flowing to the county through property taxes. This furthers the public interest in two ways: 1) by collecting back taxes owed; and 2) by returning the property to the tax rolls by placing it into the hands of those who do pay their taxes. In this manner, the county collects past revenue and ensures future revenue.

Which States Offer Tax Sales?

You could crisscross the United States going to tax sale auctions in every corner of the country. There are 35 states that auction off real estate through tax sales. If you don't like what's offered in one state, you could go to the next. You could even look for that dream vacation home on the beach in Hawaii or on a lake in upper Michigan. The possibilities are endless.

I've compiled a list of the states that offer real estate for sale at the tax sale. Some states, labeled with an asterisk (*), offer both tax lien certificates and tax sales. Usually which one they offer depends on the county. Some counties prefer tax lien certificates and others prefer tax sales. Any state that is not listed below offers only tax lien certificates and does not sell the real estate at tax sales.

1.	Alaska	13.	Louisiana *	25.	Oregon
2.	Arkansas	14.	Maine	26.	Penn.
3.	Calif.	15.	Massachusetts	27.	S. Carolina
4.	Conn. *	16.	Michigan	28.	Tennessee
5.	Del.	17.	Minnesota	29.	Texas
6.	Florida *	18.	Montana *	30.	Utah
7.	Georgia	19.	New Mexico	31.	Vermont *
8.	Hawaii	20.	Nevada	32.	Virginia
9.	Idaho	21.	New York	33.	Wash.
10.	Illinois	22.	N. Carolina	34.	Wash., DC *
11.	Indiana *	23.	N. Dakota	35.	Wisconsin
12.	Kansas	24.	Ohio *		

* These states offer both tax sales and tax lien certificates.

Why Doesn't Everyone and Their Mother Go to Tax Sales?

If tax sales are as good as I say they are, why aren't more people bidding on the properties? First of all, very few people know about tax sales. Second, there is a lack of information about tax sales. Many people don't have any idea how to go about buying tax sale properties. And even if they do know about tax sales, they don't know how to find, research, and bid on tax sales. Finally, there is the fear of the unknown.

In your hands is the knowledge for you to jump the line and build wealth. You won't be hindered by barriers like others out there. With the right knowledge, tools, and skills, you will be able to buy properties at tax sales at a fraction of their value.

Myths About Tax Sales

There are many myths about tax sales. These myths are untrue and keep people away from tax sales. Often, these myths are spread by well-meaning but uninformed individuals. Maybe they only heard something and are trying to be helpful by passing it on. Ultimately, however, they are only keeping honest, hardworking people from achieving their goals. I'm going to debunk these myths and set you in the right direction.

One myth says that only select individuals get to buy at tax sales. This is false. There is no secret group of people that get all the good properties. Tax sales are open to the public and have a transparent and open bidding system that allows anyone to participate…and you can too!

Another myth says that the properties are hard to find. This may be a problem for those who don't know how or where to look, but I'll show you exactly how to find tax sale properties.

The most common myth is that you can't do anything with a tax sale property for a year after you purchase it. This is completely false. You OWN the property. You can do whatever you want with it. You can build on it, rent it out, live in it, or sell it.

Another myth is that you can't transfer the property until a year after you purchase it. This is not true either. With a tax sale, it is true that you cannot obtain title insurance until you clear title. With this book, however, you will be on your way to clearing title much sooner than those who don't know these little known secrets.

Yet another myth is that the previous owner has the right to buy back the property from you. This is false. The right of a foreclosed owner to buy back the property after a foreclosure sale is called the right of redemption. In a tax sale, however, the previous owner does not have the right of redemption, as he may have after a foreclosure sale. The law is very clear about tax sales; the previous owner has no right of redemption after the property is sold at a tax sale. This myth came about from people confusing foreclosures with tax sales. The rights of the previous owner, however, are different in each case.

What About Tax Lien Certificates?

There is a lot of confusion between tax lien certificates (which are more well known) and tax sales. Let's get on the same page about what tax lien certificates are. Tax lien certificates are another way for the county to collect on delinquent property taxes. You're buying a negotiable instrument, a promissory note secured against the real estate, which is the right to collect the money owed but not the property itself.

When a property owner is delinquent on his property taxes, the county files a tax lien against the property. The county has the ability to sell the right to collect these taxes. The county sells a tax lien certificate to a purchaser, often at auction. When the tax lien is paid off (often by the sale or refinancing of the property), the tax lien is paid off, with interest.

Tax lien certificates are a way for the county to get its money right away. With tax lien certificates, the county doesn't have to wait for the property owner to get around to paying the taxes. It can have cash now, but it foregoes the interest on that amount. The county cuts out a lot of risk in collection and passes on that risk to a purchaser, who in return for their investment receives the amount of taxes owed plus interest.

Many states sell tax lien certificates. You don't buy the property; you buy the right to collect the cash from a tax lien against the property. The tax lien is paid off when the property is sold or if you foreclose on the lien after a few years.

Why Tax Sales?

Simply put, tax sales are an easy and inexpensive way to buy real estate for a fraction of its fair market value. There are many benefits to purchasing real estate at tax sales.

Tax sales offer a minimum bid amount that is significantly less than the value of the property. Remember that a tax sale is offered after property taxes have not been paid for years. The minimum bid for the property is the amount of the delinquent taxes, plus the costs of sale. At a tax sale, you can buy property for pennies on the dollar.

Tax sales offer an abundance of properties for sale, and thousands of properties go up for sale every year. Many counties offer a sale more than once per year!

Tax sales offer a variety of property types. Under property tax, every type of real estate is taxable. At tax sales, you can buy virtually every type of real estate, including vacant land, residential homes, multi-family dwellings, time-shares, condominiums, and commercial and industrial buildings.

Sellers at tax sales are very motivated. Counties are eager to provide you a list of tax sales because they want to turn defaulted properties into productive taxpaying properties, meaning they want a new owner who will pay the property taxes. Properties are guaranteed to sell, as long the minimum bid is offered.

The transaction costs are much lower with a tax sale than other types of purchases. There are no title or escrow fees.; there are no realtor commissions to pay; and there is very little paperwork.

What Can You Do With Property You Buy at a Tax Sale?

You can buy a home to live in. Thousands of single-family residences are available at tax sales. You can buy a home for substantially less than what you would pay on the retail market.

You can buy property to hold as an investment. Some people want to purchase for long-term investment. Buying property at a tax sale will get you property for a big discount and give you a higher return on investment.

You can purchase property and immediately "flip it" by purchasing it for the purpose of an immediate resale. This allows you to make a quick return on your investment. You can make a lot of money by flipping properties, even if you sell them at a discount off the fair market value.

You can buy land and build on the property. The possibilities are endless. You can build your dream home or income property. Most of the properties at tax sales are vacant land. You can greatly increase your return on investment by buying land cheaply at a tax sale and then building on it.

You can buy rental property. Tax sales offer commercial, industrial, and multi-family properties. You can purchase these properties and rent them out. Some of the properties will come with existing tenants and immediately produce a positive cash flow and monthly income. Your rate of return on these properties will be astounding.

You can buy a vacation property. Many people are in the market for a second home. There is no cheaper venue for buying a second home for vacationing than at a tax sale.

You can buy a time-share. These are usually in resort towns. Time-shares have a deed, and each deed is considered real estate. Property taxes are due on time-shares, just as with any other parcel of real estate.

Where Is the Best Place to Buy Tax Sales?

The ideal place to buy tax sales is your local area. By sticking to your own area, you can drive by the property and can manage it easily. You will be familiar with the area to better know what is a good deal. Stay within your comfort zone before venturing into other areas. Within your local area, you will learn property values, which will help you find deals more quickly and accurately.

However, there are many reasons why you might go out of your local area. You may want vacation property or a time-share that is out of your local area. You may want more investment properties. You may live in an area that does not offer many properties at the tax sale. For all these reasons, you can research properties outside of your local area.

Meet the Cast of Characters

Let's familiarize ourselves with the people we will be dealing with at a tax sale. Each county has different departments that work together to carry out the various aspects of the tax sale.

The County Tax Collector. The first county department you will encounter is the office of the county tax collector. In most counties, this department conducts the tax sale auction. From the tax collector's office you will get your list of properties. We'll get into how to do that later in this book. Many counties combine this office with the County Treasurer's Office.

The County Tax Assessor. This county department appraises the property and comes up with an assessed value. Keep in mind that the assessed value may seldom have anything to do with the fair market value. With this value, the county tax assessor will calculate the amount of property taxes due against the property.

The County Sheriff. In some counties, the county sheriff conducts the tax sale. In these cases, the county sheriff has the authority to seize the property and offer it for sale at the tax sale.

The County Recorder. This department holds the county records. This is where the tax deed will be recorded after you purchase a property from the tax sale. Many counties combine this office with the County Clerk Office.

The County Courthouse. In some counties, the county courthouse is where public records are held, such as real estate deed records. Some tax sales are held on the courthouse steps.

Can I Buy Directly from the County Without the Tax Sale?

Generally, you cannot purchase tax-defaulted properties directly from the county. However, there are three exceptions where you may be able to buy real estate directly from the county without going through an auction. The county must first offer the properties to the general public through a public auction at a tax sale. If a property does not sell at the public auction, it may be sold under an exception.

The first exception is for nonprofit organizations to buy property directly from the county without going through a public auction. Certain nonprofit organizations are allowed to purchase property directly from the county, outside of tax sale auctions. Usually, this is for nonprofit organizations that provide low-income housing or housing for disabled persons. However, other nonprofits may be able to buy properties in this manner.

The second exception is for land that may be unmarketable, except to adjacent property owners. The county contacts the owners adjacent to the property by mail to offer the property for sale. Factors that may lead to a property's unmarketability include the size of the lot, the lot's dimensions, and the shape of the lot. Often, the adjacent owner can merge the two lots to create a larger lot.

The third exception allows other government agencies to purchase properties from the county outside of a public auction. This exception, however, will not apply to anyone reading this book, unless you represent a government agency.

How Does Buying Property at Tax Sales Compare to Buying Property at Foreclosure Auctions?

Tax sales and foreclosures are a comparable way to purchase property. In each case, a property is financially distressed and sold through a public auction. So which way is better to acquire property? Let's take a closer look.

Tax sales are cheaper. Generally, the opening bid is lower at tax sales than at foreclosures. The opening bid at a tax sale begins at the amount of property taxes in default plus sale costs. This can range from $100 up to a few thousand dollars. Foreclosures, on the other hand, have an opening bid equal to the amount required to pay off the balance of the mortgage, which is often in the tens of thousands—if not hundreds of thousands or millions—of dollars.

Tax sales have fewer title issues. The title you get at a tax sale is superior to that of a foreclosure. At a tax sale, you get the property with ALL liens and encumbrances—including every trust deed—wiped out. At a foreclosure sale, you get the property, subject to all senior liens (liens that take priority over the lien being foreclosed). This means that if you buy a foreclosed property from the second trust deed, you still have the first trust deed to pay off. Besides other trust deeds, other monetary liens that were recorded prior to the foreclosed lien remain against the property.

With tax sales, you are helping the community. Counties benefit rather than corporations. You can feel like a good citizen by knowing your money is going to the county and state to pay for public services, rather than a private investor. Through tax sales, the county has more funds for schools, roads, and social programs.

Tax sales offer an advantage to the knowledgeable buyer. Fewer people know about tax sales, so it's easier to get properties. There is a lot of confusion and misinformation going around about tax sales. Most people have heard about tax lien certificates but don't know about tax sales.

Tax sales are abundant, and thousands of properties are up for sale every year at tax sales. It will be worth your time to get in on these bargains, and there are plenty of properties to go around for everyone.

Disadvantages of foreclosures:
1. Senior liens remain on the property after the sale.
2. The opening bid is higher than with tax sales.
3. There is a lot of competition from other buyers.

How Does Buying Property at Tax Sales Compare to Buying Property at HUD Auctions?

For those of you who have heard of HUD auctions, I'm here to tell you that tax sales are much better. Tax sales are cheaper, offer more types of properties, and have fewer title issues.

First I'll explain how a home gets to a HUD auction. The Federal Department of Housing and Urban Development (HUD) guarantees the lender of homes up to four units through the Federal Housing Administration (FHA). FHA doesn't lend the money; they just guarantee the funds if the lender has to foreclose and take the property back. If the lender forecloses and someone buys the property at the foreclosure sale, the FHA does not pay the lender anything.

If no one bids and the lender takes the property back at the foreclosure sale, the FHA pays the lender off on the balance of the loan. When the FHA pays off the loan, the title to the property is transferred to HUD. In turn, HUD sells the property at a public auction to recoup its guaranteed funds. This is the HUD auction.

HUD is able to set the opening bid on a property at whatever it decides. The guidelines only state that a property should go for market value. Watchers of HUD auctions note that the opening bid price is usually very low.

In my experience, a HUD auction bid price shoots up and the property usually sells for close to its market value. Everyone thinks they can get a bargain, but it usually doesn't turn out that way. Because of this, there isn't much of a discount for HUD homes.

Another problem with HUD auctions is that FHA only guarantees loans on condominiums, single-family residences, and dwellings with up to four units. FHA does not guarantee loans on commercial, industrial, multi-family units of five or more, vacant land, or timeshares. Thus, the types of properties available at the HUD auction are limited.

The title you get from a HUD home is no better than the one you get at a foreclosure auction. The title you get at a tax sale, however, is superior to that of a HUD home.

Disadvantages of HUD auctions:
1. High opening bid
2. Only one to four residential units are available.
3. There is too much competition from other bidders.
4. Title issues such as mechanic's liens and other encumbrances

Chapter 2

The Treasure Hunt Is Afoot: Finding Tax Sales

Chapter Overview

In this chapter, you will learn the following:

Where to get lists of tax sale properties

Introduction

One of the most common questions that I get is, "How do I get the tax sale list?" Finding out about tax sales isn't hard. You just have to know where to look. In this chapter, I'll show you where to get a list of properties for sale.

Luckily for us, counties are required to post notices of pending tax sales. The law requires counties to advertise tax sales in the newspaper at least three times. But tax sale information is also available on the Internet and at the tax collector's office.

The Newspaper

At the very least, counties are required by law to post a list of tax sale properties in a newspaper of general circulation in that county. The great thing about this is that you can get the information for the cost of the newspaper.

In the newspaper, the county will publish the dates of the sale, addresses, assessors' parcel numbers, descriptions of the properties for sale, and the opening bid price of each property. This list of properties isn't just advertised once; it must be advertised at least three times.

The newspaper in which the properties are advertised differs from county to county. It all depends on which newspaper is considered a newspaper of general circulation in that county. You can find out from the county tax collector which newspaper is used to publish tax sales and when the information will be published.

The Internet

Lists of tax sale properties are also available on the Internet. County tax collector websites provide lists of properties for sale and the dates of their tax sales. These websites also should give you updates on which properties have been removed from tax sales.

You can copy and paste these property lists on your computer for easy access. Some counties even offer lists in Microsoft$^©$ Excel spreadsheets. If this option is available, take advantage of it. With such a spreadsheet, you can easily delete properties you aren't interested in or ones that have been taken off the tax sale list. Additionally, you can make notes about each property in the spreadsheet.

Some auctions are conducted by third-party Internet auction sites. The most common is Bid4Assets.com, but eBay.com also conducts tax sale auctions. Check these Internet auction sites regularly for upcoming tax sales. It's free to get on their email list to be automatically notified of upcoming tax sale auctions.

The great thing about the tax sales on the internet is that the information is available for free and it is easy to download and customize the list on your computer.

The Tax Collector's Office

In addition to publishing the dates and list of properties in the newspaper, counties also make available for sale a copy of the list of properties at the tax collector's office.

You may find that many of the properties on the list are no longer offered for sale at the tax sale. They may have been redeemed or otherwise removed from the list of properties. You must update your list periodically with the county tax collector. Another downside is that the counties often charge a fee for the list.

Chapter 3

Ownership: What Kind of Title Do You Get?

Chapter Overview

In this chapter, you will learn the following:

1. Why the title of the property is important
2. Specific laws about tax sale titles
3. Which liens and encumbrances remain on the property after the tax sale
4. The differences between tax sale and foreclosure titles
5. The differences between tax sale and HUD auction titles
6. Which rights the previous owner has in the property after the tax sale

Introduction

When you buy a property at a tax sale, you should know which liens, trust deeds, or people can claim ownership to the property. These issues all relate to the property's title. With tax sales, that answer is easy. In this chapter, I discuss the kind of title you get from a tax sale.

The good news is the law is on your side. The laws relating to tax sales make them friendly to the buyer. They're written to encourage the purchase of property at a tax sale by giving preferential treatment to the tax liens that are being foreclosed upon.

Tax liens are treated differently than any other type of lien. A lien is a claim, or encumbrance on a property for payment of some debt, obligation, or duty. Tax liens are given greater priority in payment as opposed to other types of liens when there is a default. "Priority" determines which liens get paid first when a property is sold. Tax liens move to the front of the line when property taxes are in default. No other type of lien has priority over tax liens, but as we'll see, even tax liens have a lien priority.

Like trust deeds, ordinary liens against real estate are paid in order of their priority. In case of a default of one of the liens, the liens are paid in order of the date that they are recorded against the property. The lien that is recorded first has priority over a lien that is recorded later. Liens can be given an order of first, second, third position, and so on. A lien that has priority over another lien is said to be in senior position. A lien that has a lower priority is said to be in junior position.

Tax liens, however, have what's called super-priority. Even though a tax lien is recorded against a property later than existing liens, the law says that a tax lien has priority over private liens. This is true of all tax liens, whether they're for property taxes, state income taxes, or federal income taxes.

For example, let's say a trust deed (mortgage) is recorded in the county recorder's office on January 1. A judgment lien is filed on February 1. The trust deed has priority over the judgment lien that is filed later. However, if a tax lien is filed on March 1, the tax lien has priority over both the trust deed and the judgment lien.

The importance of priority is that at a foreclosure of a lien against real estate, the liens that are junior to the foreclosing lien are wiped out.

In our example, in a foreclosure of the trust deed, the judgment lien is wiped out. However, if the property goes to the tax sale, both the trust deed and the judgment lien are wiped out.

What the Law Says About Title

After a tax sale, you own the property free and clear of all private monetary liens. These monetary liens include all deeds of trust (mortgages), mechanic's liens, judgment liens, state tax liens, and federal tax liens (if the Internal Revenue Service is properly notified).

After buying a property at a tax sale, you will receive a tax deed. The tax deed will come from either the state or county. At the tax sale, you will not get the title from the previous owner, with all its potential flaws. You will get a superior title at the tax sale. In fact, you often get a better title than the previous owner had because it will be free from any unrecorded deeds or other defects in title.

What Remains on Title

State law tells you what remains on title after the tax sale. Later, I'll explain how to research these items so you'll know which other liens and encumbrances you will be responsible for. Generally, the following liens remain on the property after you buy it at the tax sale:

1) County taxes that were not included in the amount fixed for presale redemption of the property.

2) Liens for taxes levied by any agency that has not consented to the sale. Different taxing authorities—such as cities, water districts, school districts, and redevelopment agencies—have rights to property taxes.

3) Easements, servitudes, and water rights for which title is separately held, and restrictions of record. An easement may be for a driveway access or a utility easement for power lines. A servitude may be a right to enter the land to access another property. Water rights or oil, gas, or mineral rights have a title that is held separately from the title to the underlying property. A tax sale does not extinguish these separately held property rights.

4) Unaccepted, recorded, and irrevocable offers of dedication to a public entity. This typically takes the form of a property owner who dedicates part of his or her property to the city for a road.

State Tax Liens

When an individual owes state taxes, the state can file a tax lien against all property that the person owns in his or her county. The state tax lien is filed in the county records. This becomes a lien against the property.

When a property is sold at a tax sale and there is a state tax lien against the property, the state income tax lien is extinguished after the tax sale. The new owner of the property will not have to pay off the state tax lien.

The state will have purposely extinguished its own income tax lien against the property sold at the tax sale. This is done to facilitate and encourage the purchase of tax-defaulted property.

Federal Tax Liens

As long as the county sends a letter to the IRS notifying it of the tax sale, the IRS will have the right of redemption to buy a property that was sold at a tax sale for 120 days after the tax sale. After the 120-day period, the right of the IRS to purchase the property is extinguished and the IRS loses the right to purchase the property. The law allows the IRS to step into the shoes of the purchaser at the tax sale. For this scenario to occur, the IRS must have filed a federal tax lien in the county recorder's office at least 30 days prior to the tax sale.

The IRS, however, very rarely redeems real estate, as the ownership of real estate imposes duties and responsibilities on the owner. The federal government does not have the resources to comply with those duties and responsibilities. Furthermore, the liability of owning real estate is high for the federal government, which is the ultimate deep pocket for potential lawsuits.

If there is a federal tax lien against a property, don't worry too much about it. I've never seen the IRS redeem a property from a tax sale. Believe me when I say that 99% of the time the IRS will not redeem a property. The other 1% of the time, you'll get your money back from the purchase, plus interest. The IRS pays the tax sale purchaser the amount that he or she paid for the property. You won't make any money, but at least you won't lose any. You'll be made whole from an IRS buyback.

The law says that in order to redeem a property after a tax sale (or any similar sale), the IRS must pay the purchaser 1) the purchase price of the property; 2) interest at 6% per annum from the date of sale; and 3) the expenses of the property over the income from the property. This means that in the highly unlikely event that the IRS redeems the property, you will get all of your money back that you spent on the property, plus interest.

If the county does not properly notify the IRS of the tax sale, the federal tax lien will not be discharged by the tax sale. This does not happen in reality, because there must be

23

a federal tax lien recorded with the county recorder's office at least 30 days before the tax sale. In such a case, the county will see the tax lien and mail a certified letter to the IRS. This will comply with the notice, and then the IRS will only have the right to redeem the property for the first 120 days after the tax sale.

Chapter 4

Do Your Homework: Researching Tax Sales

Chapter Overview

In this chapter, you will learn the following:

1. The importance of researching each property before you bid at the tax sale auction
2. Why and how to gain a business relationship with a title company
3. How to read a property profile
4. How to research zoning and building issues
5. How to perform additional research, if desired

Introduction

Okay, here's the scenario: The county tax sale is coming up. You have the dates of the tax sale. You have a list of properties that will be sold at the tax sale. Now what do you do?

Once you have a list of properties, it's time to narrow down the properties you want to bid on. You will not be interested in all of the properties. Some will be unusable land. Some will be houses that need more work than you are willing to do or work that is not financially feasible to complete. Some will come with problems that you don't want to deal with. All properties are sold in "as is" condition. So a little homework is needed before you decide which properties you want to bid on.

In tax sales, the doctrine of "Buyer beware" is all-important. You will <u>not</u> get your money back on a property because of a defect or poor physical condition of the property. You bought it; you own it. This is also true of a deposit you place on a property. You won't get that money back. There are no refunds. So you have to know what you are buying, as best you can, <u>before</u> you bid at the tax sale.

The only time that you will ever get your money back from a tax sale is if the tax deed is void or the property should not have been sold in the first place. This almost never happens.

Meet Your Local Title Company

A close relationship with a title company is a must for any real estate buyer, especially a buyer of tax sales. You will need the information that a title company can provide.

Your first step is to introduce yourself to a title company and try to have a title representative (called a title rep) assigned to you. To do this, call a title company and inform them that you are a real estate investor and that you plan on being a good customer of the title company. Explain that you would like to have a title rep assigned to you. Meet with your title rep and explain how you plan to acquire properties at tax sales.

The title rep will give you invaluable services. She should give you resources such as an Internet account to access the title company's website to investigate properties. She also should give you access to the customer service department, which will give you property profiles.

If the title rep doesn't explain how the business works, let me. The mutual benefit comes from a title rep giving you title services and you giving your title business to her. Title reps work on salary plus commission for each title policy they sell. She will get credit for every title order you place with the title company. She won't charge you for these invaluable services, as long as you give her your title business. If anyone off the street asked for a property profile, a title company might charge $75 for *each* property profile. In the next section, I'll explain what information you can get through a property profile.

Let your rep know you will be purchasing property at a county tax sale. Find out what the title company will require to issue a title insurance policy. Also find out the costs of clearing title and issuing a title insurance policy against the property.

Property Profile

Now that you have a title rep, you can get a property profile for each property you are interested in. It's best to get these profiles online. This will pose the least inconvenience to the title company and save a lot of paper and time. There are three major documents in a property profile that you will use to determine if the property is worth further research. These three documents are the cover page, the assessor's parcel map, and comparable sales.

The Cover Page

The cover page includes the name of the owner of the property, their mailing address, the address of the property, the property's assessor's parcel number, the size of the lot, and the current use of the property (vacant, commercial, single family residential, etc.). Often, the cover page shows the last sale of the property with the date of sale, the sale price, and the loan amount. If the property is a single-family residence, the cover page will show the number of bedrooms and bathrooms, the livable square footage, and the year built. You usually can get the cover page online when you get an account to access the title company's website.

A word of warning: The cover page is not always up to date with the latest information on the property. Unpermitted additions to a property do not show in the public information. You will have to actually visit the property to make sure there is still a building there!

For example, if you're in the market for a residential property, you can look at the cover page and eliminate any property that is not a single-family residence. If you need a four-bedroom home, you can eliminate any property that is not a four-bedroom single-family residence. You can qualify and disqualify property based on any of the criteria given in the cover sheet.

The Assessor's Parcel Map

The property profile also includes the assessor's parcel map (I'll call them parcel maps from now on). To locate the subject property on the parcel map, first look at the assessor's parcel number. The first digits are the book number. The middle digits are the tract number. The last digits are the parcel number. The parcel numbers are the circled numbers on the parcel map.

Let's look at an example of a parcel map in Appendix A. There you will find two maps. On the first map, look for parcel number 0279-122-11. It is in Book 279, page 12, section 2, parcel 11. Would you buy this lot? It is about 97 feet wide and more than 9,000 square feet in area. However, how do you access the property? Notice that it is landlocked and has no access to the street. Besides access problems, how would you get utilities to the property without a utility easement from an adjacent landowner?

Let's try another example. On the second map, look for parcel 0280-231-46. Would you buy it at a tax sale? What could you do with that lot? Notice the width of the lot. Is it wide enough to build on? This lot is 20 feet wide. With side setbacks, you may be able to build a house that is 5 feet wide. Building a livable home on this property is not feasible. Now you see how important it is to research a property before you bid.

The parcel map shows the shape and dimensions of the lot, major easements across the property, neighboring properties, and the location of nearby streets. This is vital information. Sometimes the parcel map will tell you that the lot you are interested in is in the middle of a street. Or it will show that utility easements traverse the property and you can't build on it.

There are limits to parcel maps. They will not show you whether the property is on a hillside or whether the property is a big drainage ditch. You will have to find out this information from a drive-by.

Comparable Sales

The property profile offers comparable sales information. This is recent sales information for properties that are comparable to the subject property. Later in this chapter, I discuss how to use this information to determine what the property is worth. But know for now that you can get this information from a property profile.

Online Resources

Many online resources allow you to gather information about a property you are researching. I list some of these below.

Zillow.com: This website gives a great deal of free information about properties and also approximates their value. I have found Zillow.com to be a good guide when figuring out the value of properties.

Trulia.com: This website gives real estate market information and allows you to access sales information for properties.

Google.com: Google Maps allows you to view a photo of the front of the property and offers directions to and from the property. Remember that the photograph of the front of the property may have been taken a while ago and may not reflect the current condition of the property.

RealtyTrak.com: This website gathers information about real estate sales, including historical data.

Realtor.com: This website is used by licensed real estate agents and brokers who are members of the National Association of Realtors. This site allows you to browse the Multiple Listing System to gather historical sales information to help determine property values.

Loopnet.com: This website gives a great deal of free information about commercial and industrial properties. You can research comparables and see what other commercial and industrial properties are going for in the area.

Researching Land

The Drive-by

A drive-by will reveal a great deal of information to help you determine whether it is feasible to buy vacant land. For example, you will discover the contours of the land. The flatter the land, the easier it will be to build on. You will see whether the street is completed—for instance, whether there is a curb, gutter, and sidewalk. You will know whether there is a sewer manhole in the middle of the street, which will indicate whether there is a sewer in the street. If there is no sewer, are you allowed to put in a septic system? Similarly, you will see service covers for gas, water, electricity, and phone service. Or maybe telephone or power poles are on the street. If the utilities are not there, you'll have to put them in as the developer of the property.

The Building and Safety Department

At the building and safety department, check your local building codes. Specifically ask about the property's setback requirements. The setbacks will tell you the dimensions of the buildable area of the lot. If the lot is very narrow you'll have to build a very narrow house.

To illustrate the importance of building setbacks, let's assume you are researching a vacant lot. If you know the dimensions of the lot from the assessor's parcel map that came with the property profile and you know the building setbacks from the building department, then you will know how large (or how small) of a building you can build on that lot. For example, if a lot is 50 feet wide and the side setbacks are 10 feet on each side, you can only build a house that is a maximum of 30 feet wide. I've seen lots for sale that are only three feet wide—you couldn't build anything on it.

The Planning Department

Zoning will tell you which types of building you can build on a vacant lot. These buildings can include single-family residences, duplexes, triplexes, four-plexes, and multi-family units, as well as retail, commercial, office-commercial, light industrial, and heavy industrial buildings.

Environmental Health

The environmental health department will tell you whether any pending or final environmental hazards are registered against the property. This department also will tell whether you are required to install a septic system if there is not a sewer main next to the property.

Researching Residential Property

The Drive-by

You should physically inspect every property you plan to bid on at the tax sale. A drive-by will tell you all kinds of information. You'll know whether the three-bedroom, two-bath house is still standing on the property that the cover sheet of the property profile told you was there. You will know whether the property is occupied or vacant. If it is occupied, you'll know that the property is in livable condition, even if it might need some repairs. However, you'll have the tenant's right to possession and an eviction to deal with.

You'll know the condition of the neighborhood. Do the neighbors take pride in ownership? Do you see many vacant and boarded-up properties? Is the neighborhood all vacant land? Is it a very nice neighborhood? Are there a lot of "for sale" signs in the neighborhood indicating an exodus?

The Planning Department

At the planning department, you can check the zoning of the property. This will tell you the current zoning of the property and the current use of the property, which may not be the same. Since the single-family residence was built, the zoning may have changed to commercial. In such a case, it is normal for an existing house to be allowed to continue as a non-conforming use, as long as it is not vacant for one year. If the property becomes vacant for one year, then typically the house must be converted to commercial.

Code Enforcement

The code enforcement department will tell you whether there are any pending actions against the property. Code enforcement enforces the building codes. If a property is slated for condemnation and demolition, the code enforcement department will always be intimately involved. The code enforcement department also will tell you whether there are any liens against the property for substandard conditions. In such a case, there will be physical corrections to be made to the property and fees to pay.

Go to City Hall

You must look into the regulatory aspects of the property. The two most important departments to visit are: 1) building and safety; and 2) planning. While you are at city hall, you also may want to visit the code enforcement and environmental health departments.

Go to the County Recorder or Courthouse

Every county holds records of recorded liens against real estate in the county recorder's office or at the county courthouse. You can check for liens against a property at the county's recorder office or county courthouse, and you can get a copy of the actual lien. Each recorder's office holds its records in a different way.

Many counties have a computer-searchable index of properties. Some even allow you to search county records online. However, these searches only tell you whether there is a lien; they won't give you a copy of the lien.

Another common way for counties to hold indexes of documents against properties is through microfiche, which often are available at the recorder's office or courthouse. Ask the clerk how to search for liens against a property via microfiche.

What's the Property Worth?

Determine the fair market value for the property. The most common way to determine this is to look at comparable sales (called comps in the industry). Good comps will be properties within a mile of the subject property that are similar in size and amenities and that have sold within the last year. This is what real estate appraisers do to find the value of property; they gather comps.

For vacant land, you can check on other land sales in the area and see how much a similar-sized parcel is selling for in the area. You also can check to see approximately how much per acre or square foot the land is selling for in the area. Then you can determine the value of the property you are interested in.

Be sure to compare apples to apples. When determining the value of land, compare commercial property with other commercial property. Make sure as well that you compare single-family residential property to single-family residential property. For a quality comparison, you would not compare multi-family property to industrial property.

Sometimes comps are hard to find. I've often come across property that is unique in the area, and I've seen property where there have been no recent sales nearby. In these cases you'll have to expand your search of comps to other neighborhoods or go back further into the past to find sales. A property that is merely listed for sale or pending in escrow but not yet sold is not a good comp.

Survey

If you're overly cautious or have extra time and money on your hands, you can do a little extra research about the property you are interested in. This research is not always necessary, but it will give you the peace of mind that you have been exhaustive in your due diligence.

You can get a survey of the property, which will tell you the true corners of the lot. If there's a great deal of vacant land in the area, it can be nearly impossible to tell which lot you are buying. The only way to tell for sure is to obtain a survey. A survey, however, will cost you approximately $1,200 or more.

PART II
Winning Strategies for Success at Tax Sales

Chapter 5

The Early Bird Gets the Worm: How to Buy Property Before the Tax Sale

Chapter Overview

In this chapter, you will learn the following:

1. The strategy behind purchasing property before the tax sale
2. Which properties pay off the most
3. How to contact the owner
4. How to purchase the property from the owner
5. How to redeem the property.

Introduction

Did you ever think about buying a property before the tax sale? Waiting for a property to come to auction and then bidding on the property against other bidders is only one way to buy property at the tax sale. Another way to buy property is to purchase it from the owner before the tax sale.

How Do You Buy Property Before the Tax Sale?

It's an easy concept, really. In a nutshell, you contact the owner of the property that is on the tax sale list. Then you negotiate the purchase of the property. Once you own the property, you can redeem it (pay off the back property taxes owed) and take it off the auction block.

If the owner does not pay off the back property taxes, he will lose the property to the tax sale auction. If you purchase the property before the tax sale, you won't have to bid against other buyers at the auction. It's a win-win situation if you structure it right. You're helping the owner save the property from the auction block and paying the owner some money. You'll buy the property for less than market value to ensure that you make some money. Then you take over the property and redeem it from the tax collector.

What Are the Potential Pitfalls?

Buying property before the tax sale can be very profitable. However, you'll need to look out for a few things to avoid making costly mistakes. Be sure to avoid these pitfalls.

Make sure that you get an owner's title insurance policy. An owner's title insurance policy ensures that the seller is the true owner of the property and discloses all of the liens and encumbrances against the property. Another potential problem is dealing with someone that is not really the owner of the property or not all of the owners.

Make sure you are aware of all of the costs of purchasing the property. When you buy the property without title insurance or without a closing agent, such as an escrow company or closing attorney, you run the risk of not being aware of all of the liens against the property. Research the title thoroughly and follow up on the balance of all liens.

If possible, go through escrow or a closing attorney when purchasing the property. Sometimes you may not have the time if the tax sale is coming up fast. Or you may be short on funds to close. However, I must reiterate that it is important to do the transaction right, or pass it up. Ideally, you should work with some type of closing agent.

The Types of Properties to Look For

Not every property is ripe for the picking. You must be selective about which properties you are interested in and which to avoid.

The best kinds of properties are ones in which the owner lives out of town. Why is that the case? Absentee owners are more likely to want to get rid of the property. The property may be an eyesore or more hassle than it's worth. This can create motivation for the owner to sell—and at a cheap price.

Remember that you'll have to pay off any liens against the property. More liens will increase the purchase price of the house. For example, let's say you're interested in a certain property. The opening bid is $5,000. The balance of the liens against the property totals $90,000. The property is worth $120,000. While you may be able to buy the property for less than $10,000 at the tax sale auction, you will not be able to buy it for less than $95,000 from the owner.

Look for properties within your price range. If you can't afford the opening bid price, you won't have the money to redeem the property. So pick properties you can afford.

Stay away from any property that you would not bid on at the auction. Do not pursue any lot that is too small to build on, or a house in need of extensive repairs that would put you in over your head. Keep in mind that if any liens against the property are also in foreclosure, you'll have to cure those defaults as well as the tax sale.

Contacting the Owner

From what you gathered to find and research tax sales, you will have all the information you need to pursue buying the property before the tax sale.

First, write a letter to the owner offering to purchase the property. The property profile will give you the owner's name and mailing address. A handwritten letter is the best way to get the owner to read the letter. A form letter or word-processed letter is less likely to be read and is thus less likely to get you a response. But you can cut and paste the letter if you are writing a lot of them. You can find a sample letter in Appendix A.

Negotiating the Purchase

Once you get a positive response from your letter, you'll want to meet with the owner. Be friendly and positive. Try to meet at the property, even if it is vacant land.

Remember to be sensitive to the owner's situation. The owner may be afraid, embarrassed, angry, or ignorant, or who knows what else. Use some diplomacy and understanding in dealing with the owner, but don't let the owner take advantage of you.

Gather as much information as possible about the property. Inquire about the condition of the property and ask whether any repairs are needed. If the land is vacant, ask where the utilities are or if there has ever been a building there.

To come up with an offer on the property, first determine the costs you will incur and which liens you will have to take over. These are the hard costs of the property. Then determine how much the owner is willing to take to save the property from the tax sale. Sometimes this is just a few thousand dollars...maybe less. A good rule of thumb is to buy the property for less than 70% of the property's actual value.

After successfully negotiating the purchase of the property, you'll want to close on the deal. Have a real estate professional draw up a purchase agreement. With that purchase agreement, get a closing agent such as an escrow company or closing attorney to handle the transaction. Make sure to get title insurance, too.

Redeeming the Property

After closing on the purchase, you'll need to redeem the property by paying off the past due property taxes. You must contact the tax collector to make arrangements to pay off the back property taxes. This will take the property off the tax-defaulted properties list and remove it from the tax sale.

When you pay the back property taxes, get a receipt. You can pay off the back property taxes in full, or you can make arrangements to pay them off in installment payments.

Be mindful of the deadline to redeem the property. Call the tax collector and find out the last day to redeem the property. After the property has gone to the auction block, it will be too late for you to redeem the property.

Chapter 6

Get Ahead of the Pack: Prepare for the Auction

Chapter Overview

In this chapter, you will learn the following:

1. How to register for the tax sale auction
2. How to place a deposit for the tax sale, if required
3. How to choose your title and vesting
4. How to monitor the list of available properties
5. How to pay for the property when you're the winning bidder
6. How the auction is conducted
7. How to prepare before the auction

Introduction

By now, you'll have done your homework. You'll have a list of the properties for sale at the tax sale auction. You'll have researched the properties you are interested in. You'll have narrowed down the list of properties you plan to bid on. Now it's time to get ready for the auction.

Register for the Auction

To bid on properties at the tax sale, you first must register as a bidder. Only registered bidders can buy properties at the tax sale.

If the auction is offered online, go to the website and register online. If the auction is offered as a live auction or sealed bid auction, obtain the registration material from the county tax collector. It will be available online at the county tax collector's website or at the county tax collector's office.

Register as early as possible for the auction, as soon as you know when the auction will be held. Each auction has its own registration deadlines. <u>Don't wait; always register early</u>.

Placing a Deposit

As part of the registration process, some auctions require you to place a deposit with the county. Note that not all auctions require a bid deposit. The purpose of the deposit is to make sure that only serious buyers bid on the properties. You will forfeit this deposit if you are the winning bidder at the auction and you do not complete the purchase of the property.

The deposit is refundable if you aren't the successful bidder for any properties. If you place a deposit and you are not the winning bidder for any of the properties you bid on, the county will refund your deposit in full. So you get your deposit back if you don't win any auctions, but your deposit will go toward the purchase price of any properties for which you are the winning bidder.

Deposits are most often required with Internet auctions, since the nature of the Internet allows anonymity. Many people will participate in an Internet auction where they don't have to deal with other bidders face-to-face. Unfortunately, this also invites bidders who are not serious about the auction. Deposits are a good way to keep only the serious bidders in the auction.

The deposit is typically $500. However, with very high priced properties, the deposit requirement can be higher. I've seen a bid deposit requirement of $100,000 for a property with an opening bid of $1.2 million (it was hundreds of acres of woodland worth many times that).

There are many ways to place your deposit. Each way takes a different amount of time. For example, if you pay by personal check, it may take several business days for your deposit to be processed while your check clears. If you pay cash, your deposit will be recognized immediately. To place a deposit, you can do any of the following:

1. Bring cash to the tax collector's office
2. Bring a cashier's check to the tax collector's office
3. Bring a personal check to the tax collector's office
4. Make a credit card payment over the Internet
5. Make an "e-check" payment over the Internet.

Title and Vesting

As part of the registration process, the county will ask you what title and vesting to place on the tax sale deed. This determines how you will take ownership of the property. The title is the name of the purchaser, and the vesting describes the form of ownership. The county will not give you advice on which form of ownership to take.

For the title, use the name of the individual or business entity. If you're taking title as an individual, it is best to use your full name. This includes your first name, middle name, last name, and any suffix. Here's an example: William Steven Jones, Sr.

There are many different ways to hold ownership of property, each with its own legal ramifications. The form of ownership may affect real property taxes, income taxes, inheritance, and gift taxes, as well as transferability of title and exposure to creditor claims. This can get complex. Consult a real estate attorney if you're at all uncomfortable with how to take title.

The form of ownership you take is most important when more than one individual owns the property. Only two vestings are important to note: 1) joint tenants; and 2) tenants in common.

Joint tenancy produces some consequences automatically. Each owner must have an equal share in the property. John must own 50% and Bill must own 50% so that each has an equal share in the property. Joint tenants have the right of survivorship, meaning that when one joint tenant dies, the other(s) automatically receives his share, by operation of law. Thus, when John dies, Bill becomes 100% owner of the property.

Tenants in common has different consequences to consider. Each owner may own a different percentage of the property. John can own 60% of the property and Bill can own 40%. Tenants in common do not have the right of survivorship. Each owner can leave his or her share to his or her own heirs.

A list of examples of ways to hold ownership of the property appears below:

Type of Ownership	Title and Vesting	Comments
An individual who has never been married	Jane Doe, a single woman	A single woman
An individual who is divorced	Jane Doe, an unmarried woman	An unmarried woman
A married couple, jointly owning property	John Doe and Jane Doe, as husband and wife	A married couple
A married woman, individually	Jane Doe, a married woman as her sole and separate property	A married woman as her property only
A corporation	ABC Corporation, a California corporation	A California corporation
A limited liability company	Newco, LLC, a California limited liability company	A California limited liability company
A partnership	123 Partnership, a California partnership	A California partnership
A trust	John Doe, trustee of the John Doe Living Trust dated January 1, 2005	Trustee of the John Doe Living Trust dated January 1, 2005
Two or more individuals who are not married, with right of survivorship	John Doe, a single man, and Bill Money, an unmarried man, as joint tenants	As joint tenants
Two or more individuals who are not married, without right of survivorship	John Doe, a single man, as to an undivided 60% interest, and Bill Money, an unmarried man, as to an undivided 40% interest, as tenants in common	As tenants in common

Monitor the List of Properties

You must continue to monitor the list of properties that are available. Many of the properties on the tax sale list will be redeemed by the owner. This means the property owner pays off the property taxes and the property is taken off the tax sale properties list. The county will publish lists of properties that are no longer for sale.

With redemptions, the owner filing bankruptcy, and other events, properties are taken off the auction block. By the time the auction comes around, some or all of the properties that you are interested in will not be available at the tax sale.

Know the minimum bid for the properties. This will not change from the time the auction is announced. Some properties will sell for the minimum bid amount.

Know the Payment Terms

Each county has its own payment terms. Payment terms are also different for live auctions, Internet auctions, and sealed bid auctions. Learn the payment terms before the auction so you'll be ready to pay for the property when your bid is accepted.

After the auction, it is common to pay for the property immediately with certified funds such as a cashier's check. However, it is also common for you to be able to pay for a property that sells for more than a certain dollar amount with an initial deposit immediately and to pay the balance within a few days.

For example, auctions commonly require a deposit of $5,000 for properties selling for more than $10,000, with the balance due within 30 days. The county, however, may require payment in full for properties that are less than $10,000. So with a live auction, you'll have to bring a $5,000 cashier's check for each property you plan to bid on that will sell for more than $10,000.

If you overpay for the property, the county will mail you a refund check for the difference. Try to avoid this, as the county will take their sweet time to mail you a check.

Know the Bidding Amounts

Find out how much you must outbid the last bid. Bids are given in set increments. It is typical to for auctions to set bid increments at a minimum of $100 up to $10,000, then to set bid increments of $1,000 after that.

For example, the opening bid for a property may be $600. You can bid $700 as the next highest bid. You can raise the bid to $700 or $2,400. However, once the bidding reach $10,000, then the next highest bid will be $11,000, not $10,100. Under the auction rules, you cannot bid $10,100.

Organize Your Bidding Strategy

Determine the maximum amount you are willing to bid on each property. This comes down to knowing how much you will bid. Figure in all costs (eviction, clearing title, deed recording and document transfer tax, cleanup and fix-up, selling costs, etc.). You may want to determine the maximum you are willing to bid on a property in relation to the property's fair market value. As a rule of thumb, most investors are willing to spend up to 70% of a property's fair market value.

When you start the bidding, always offer the minimum bid amount. Sometimes you will be the only one who bids on a particular property. If that's the case, you paid the least amount possible to buy the property.

You can bid incrementally for the property. This is where you increase the bidding by the next highest increment, often $100 for amounts less than $10,000 and then increments of $1,000 thereafter. For example, if the current bid is $800, then the next highest bid possible is $900. By bidding incrementally, you will pay the least possible for the property. However, be prepared to duke it out with another bidder who is using the same strategy. This can last a while and bid you up more than you would have paid.

Another strategy involves making a high overbid. This is where you yell out a big increase in the bid. For example, if the current bidding is at $800, you can raise your bid card and yell out $1,500, in which case the new current bid becomes $1,500. When you use this strategy, you scare off some bidders who can't compete with you. However, you also risk paying more for the property than you would if you had bid incrementally.

The Internet has allowed for a type of strategy called snipping. With snipping, you offer a bid in the last seconds of the auction. This precludes other bidders from outbidding you, because the auction will have ended. This strategy is only effective in Internet auctions, because there is a definite time at which the auction ends.

Once you know your bidding strategy for a particular property, write down the information on a bid sheet. The bid sheet should state the address and assessor's parcel number of the property, the property's auction number, the date and time of auction, and your strategy for this purchase.

Bidding strategy tips:
1. Always offer the opening bid. You may just get it.

2. Bid incrementally for the lowest possible winning bid.
3. Make a high overbid to eliminate some competition.
4. Bid at the last minute to snatch up bargains.

Go to the Bank

You will need certified funds to buy property at the tax sale. This is usually in the form of cashier's checks (some banks no longer issue cashier's checks, or only issue cashier's checks over a certain amount), but a teller's check or bank check should suffice. Cash is seldom accepted at tax sales. Be sure to check the requirements of each auction.

In general, you should make the cashier's checks out to the county tax collector (i.e., Los Angeles County Tax Collector), but check with the county's payment terms. If you make the check out to yourself, the county may not accept your endorsement on the back of the check over to the county. If you do not end up using all of your cashier's checks, your bank should allow you to turn them back in for a full refund if you return the original checks uncashed.

Get cashier's checks in these amounts:
1. $5,000
2. $3,000
3. $1,000
4. $500
5. $200
6. $100

Do not buy money orders. They often have small maximum amounts, usually about $600. They do not have to be issued by a financial institution. There are all kinds of money orders that are not certified funds. If stolen, money orders are also easier to cash by thieves.

If the auction requires a $5,000 deposit for properties valued over $10,000, you'll need a cashier's check for $5,000. If it requires payment in full for properties under $10,000, you'll need cashier's checks in the following increments: $5,000, $3,000, $1,000, $500, $200, $100. You should also have $100 in cash in small bills. This way, you can make change to buy any property and not have to overpay and get a refund.

Drive by the Auction Location

This sounds elementary, but it's really important. You'll gain familiarity by driving to the auction site. First you will know how to get there from your house. Then, you should figure out where to park. Finally, get out and walk to where the auction will be held.

Believe me—you don't want to have to figure these things out on the day of the auction, especially if you're running late. You'll have enough to worry about without increasing your stress levels. Plus, you'll have a big leg up on those who didn't familiarize themselves with the auction site.

Go to the Auction Website

Before the auction begins, familiarize yourself with the auction website. Know how to navigate the website. Read over the frequently asked questions (FAQ). Make sure you are a registered bidder for the auction. Bookmark the auction web page in your Internet browser. Know how to get to the web page that lists the properties you are interested in.

Make sure your computer is up to par. You don't want to realize that your modem isn't working the day of the auction. Disable or modify any spyware blockers, pop-up blockers, or anti-virus programs that may interfere with your bidding.

Check your Internet connection speed. You'll need as fast a connection as possible. Dial-up service is the generally the slowest and least reliable Internet connection. Make sure you don't get disconnected while online. The best at-home Internet connections are broadband services such as DSL and cable. A wired connection with an Ethernet cable is more reliable than a wireless connection.

How Tax sales Are Conducted

In the next few chapters, we'll explore what to expect at the tax sale auction itself. Tax sales are conducted in a few different ways. Each county has its own preference as to how to conduct their auctions. A variety of factors affect each county's decision. Smaller counties sometimes combine their tax sales on the same day or at the same auction. You'll have to check with the county you are interested in to find out how their auction is conducted.

Tax sale auctions often take place on a Monday. The reason for this is simple. The owner's right to pay off the back taxes and redeem the property often ends, by law, at 5 p.m. on the business day before the tax sale begins. That means that the owner must pay his or her back taxes on the previous Friday by 5 p.m.. This allows the weekend to get ready for the tax sale and prevents the owner from complaining that they had the money just last night.

Chapter 7

Going...Going...Gone: Live Auctions

Chapter Overview

In this chapter, you will learn the following:

1. How to prepare for a live tax sale auction
2. What to do at a live tax sale auction
3. How to bid at a tax sale auction
4. Strategies for live tax sale auctions
5. Etiquette at a live tax sale auction

Introduction

A live auction has to be the most thrilling of the auction methods. You will see a lot of people at the auction, and the vast majority of them will be unprepared. Most of them are looky-loos. With this book, you'll have the edge over them.

Be Ready for the Auction

The night before the auction, review your research and bidding sheets. Make sure you have your cashier's checks in the proper amounts. Make sure you have your bid card. Know which properties you will bid on and when they will appear during the auction. Make sure you have directions to the auction. Gather your materials and put them in a folder for you to take with you the next day. Get a good night's sleep; the auction can be tiring. Wear comfortable clothing and shoes to the auction.

Start your day right. Get up early to go to the auction. This is the day to have a good breakfast. If you need coffee to get the day going, take the time to have your coffee. Bring a snack with you. Don't wait until the last minute to show up at the auction. Make sure you have all of your materials before you leave the house. Leave your house early and allow extra time to get there. A traffic jam or bad weather can make your commute longer. You'll want to get a good parking space.

Checklist to prepare for the auction:
1. Property research and bid sheets
2. Cashier's checks
3. Bid card
4. Address and directions to the auction

Arriving at the Auction

When you get to the auction, position yourself well. You'll want to have a good seat. You won't want to sit on the sides where the auctioneer has to strain his neck to see you. Sit as close to front and center as possible. The seats actually fill up. It's no fun being crowded in the back of the room and standing behind other people.

Leave your cell phone or pager in the car if you can. If you must have it with you, turn it on vibrate or mute. You don't want calls, texts, and emails to distract you from your mission.

Listen carefully. Sometimes properties are taken off the auction at the last minute. Make sure you know which property is being called for auction. Do not mistakenly bid on the wrong property.

Waiting for Your Property

Live auctions auction off the properties one by one. They usually go in order of the auction list. You may have to wait a while before the property that you are interested in will be up for sale. Be patient. Do not leave the room. The auctioning can go fast sometimes.

It is hard to say how long it will take. Some properties will not have any bidders or only one bidder and the auctioneer will move on quickly. Some properties have a lot of bidders and the auctioneer will slow down. Still other properties have a couple of bidders increasing each other's bid for a long period of time. A long auction will offer breaks and lunch; use this time to go to the restroom, review your properties, or collect your thoughts.

Be patient and wait for your time to bid on the property that you want. You will definitely learn from the bidding that's taking place. Keep your eyes and ears open.

Bidding at Live Auctions

Your first bid at a live tax sale may leave you anxious. You may be nervous or even shaking a bit. There will be a lot of people around, and they will be looking at you when you hold up your bid card. Take a deep breath and relax. Don't let the scene intimidate you. Making a bid is easy. There are two ways to make a bid at a live auction. Either you can make an incremental bid, or you can yell out a high raise bid.

An incremental bid is the easier of the two. To make an incremental bid, all you have to do is hold your bid card up high when the auctioneer calls out a bid amount. He will say something like, "Do I hear 2,000?" By holding up your bid car, you are making a bid of $2,000 for that particular property.

A high raise bid involves one extra step. To make a high raise bid, hold up your bid card and call out an amount. For example, the auctioneer may say, "Do I hear 1,700?" You'll hold up your bid card and yell out, "Twenty-five hundred." The auctioneer will repeat, "Twenty-five hundred." In this example, you have increased the bid to $2,500 for that particular property.

When making a bid at a live auction, try to make eye contact with the auctioneer. Remember that by just holding up your bid card, you are making an incremental bid. If you want to make a high raise overbid, clearly yell out the amount while holding up your bid card. Be sure that the auctioneer repeats your higher bid.

Be careful with your bid card. Do not use it as a fan. Do not wave it around. Do not stretch your arms with your bid card in your hand. Do not lose it. Do not let anyone borrow it. Keep it facedown in your lap until you use it to bid on a property. You don't want to inadvertently bid on a property. Even an unintended bid is a valid bid.

Bidding Strategies

The incremental bid can keep the bidding up for a while. To bid to the next highest increment, merely show your bid card. You do not have to yell out the amount. The auctioneer will understand that you merely want to be the next highest bidder by the lowest possible amount.

A high raise bid will scare off a lot of other bidders. Again, you do this by showing the auctioneer your bid card and yelling out the bid price. Of course, you run the risk of paying more than you would have without the high bid.

Stick to your strategy. Do not bid more than your maximum bid. Do not bid more than you have in cash or cashier's check.

Second Chance

If the property you bid on goes to someone else, stick around for a while. The auction rules will require the winning bidder to pay for the property or put down a deposit. If that person does not pay for the property or put down a deposit, the property will go back up for auction immediately. The property will begin to sell for the original starting bid and the process will start over again. This actually happens a lot. By sticking around for a while after the property is initially sold, you may get a second chance at bidding on it. This is good news for you, as other bidders may have already left the auction.

I've seen a house sell for about $80,000 and then when the bidder didn't pay for the property, it went for sale at the auction again 30 minutes later. The property then sold for $17,000 since most of the other bidders had left the auction.

Winning the Auction

If you are the successful bidder at the auction...congratulations! Your work, however, is not done yet. Go and pay for the property or at least the minimum deposit right away. Be sure to get a receipt. If you don't pay for the property right away, it will be put up for re-auction. The auctioning of the next property will go on, but you can still keep bidding while you are paying for your property. Just because the next property you want to bid on is coming up next, do not let the auction you just won get away from you.

Take notice of who is bidding against you—they want to buy the property too. Maybe you could sell the property to one of your competitors at the auction for a quick cash turn-around. Approach the other bidders and get their names, phone numbers, and email addresses. See if they would be interested in buying the property from you after you get the tax sale deed from the county. You could make a good profit with very little risk by flipping the properties to your fellow bidders.

Auction Etiquette

If you are the high bidder on a property and are awarded a property, do not yell and jump up and down. You'd think I wouldn't have to mention it, but it happens. Be a gracious winner. Don't over-celebrate. You don't want to make any enemies out of the other bidders who may later try to relatiate against you by bidding up your next property.

If you lose a hotly contested bidding war, be a good loser. Don't throw a tantrum or storm out of the room. Keep your decorum and focus on the next property. Everything is a learning experience.

Chapter 8

Working at Home in Your Pajamas: Internet Auctions

Chapter Overview

In this chapter, you will learn the following:

1. How Internet tax sale auctions are conducted
2. The basics of no reserve auctions
3. What to expect at an Internet tax sale auction
4. How to bid at Internet tax sale auctions
5. Strategies for Internet tax sale auctions

Introduction

The Internet has played a significant role in county tax sales, and Internet auctions are becoming a more popular method to hold auctions. In May 2004, San Bernardino County, California sold more than 2,400 properties and raked in a record $41.7 million from its tax sale on Bid4Assets.com. Tax sales offer a low cost way for counties to sell property. More people can participate in the auction from around the globe. The cost and liability of having a lot of people in one building for a tax sale is eliminated, and counties aren't limited to room capacities as with live auctions.

The most widely used website for tax sale auctions over the Internet is bid4assets.com. However, eBay.com is gaining in popularity among tax collectors. Most likely, any tax sale you'll come across is auctioned at one of these two websites.

How Internet Tax Sale Auctions Are Conducted

In an Internet auction, a third-party provider conducts the tax sale. All properties are auctioned off over the internet. There is no live person yelling numbers. You never see the other bidders. The auctioneer is a computer.

All the county's properties are up for sale on the website. The bidding for properties starts at about the same general time. The end time of the auction for different properties stops at different times on different days. Auctions often take place over a period of days.

For example, a county may offer their tax sale from August 1 through August 5. During that time, 100 properties may be sold each day. Those hundred properties each may be split into groups of 15 properties. The group of properties may have auction closing times of 10 a.m., 10:30 a.m., 11 a.m., etc.

Benefits of Internet Auctions

Internet auction bidding is completely anonymous. No one will know your name or see your face. You don't have to drive anywhere to bid on an Internet auction. You can bid in your pajamas in your living room, at any time of the night.

You can be anywhere on the globe and bid on properties. With the worldwide reach of the Internet, you are not tied to being present at a live auction. You literally can relax on the beach while making money!

You won't have to have any performance anxiety over yelling out bids at a live auction. You don't have to be around anyone else who might try to intimidate you.

No-Reserve Auctions

There are two types of auctions: reserve and no-reserve auctions. It is easiest to explain a no-reserve auction by first explaining a reserve auction.

A reserve auction is one in which the seller of the property has told the auctioneer not to sell the property unless the bidding reaches a predetermined amount. Only the seller and the auctioneer know the reserve amount.

Once the reserve amount is reached the property will sell at the highest bid. If the reserve amount is not reached the property will not be sold, even though there is a highest bidder.

For example, say a property has an opening bid of $500, but the seller has instructed the auctioneer not to sell the property unless the bidding reaches at least $900 (the reserve amount set by the seller). If the highest bid is $700, the property will not be sold and the auctioneer will cancel the sale. If the highest bid is $1,100, then the highest bid is greater than the reserve amount and the property will be sold for $1,100.

By contrast, a no reserve auction is one in which the seller does not set a reserve amount. As long as a bidder bids at least the opening bid amount, the auctioneer will sell the property for any amount at or above the opening bid.

All tax sales are offered as no-reserve auctions. You can rest assured that once you bid at least the opening bid amount the highest bidder will buy the property.

What to Expect at Internet Auctions

Bidding can happen very quickly. Multiple people can bid on the same property at the same time, and you wouldn't know it. People can bid 24 hours a day. The auction does not close until the auction expiration for each particular property, with extended time if any. I'll explain extended time later.

Properties are offered up to a certain date and time at which time the auction expires. Once the deadline is reached and all bidding has ended, the property will be awarded to the highest bidder, if there are any bidders.

During the auction, some properties will be removed from the auction. They can be removed when the owner files bankruptcy before the sale or due to other events. You may find that a property that you bid on is taken off the auction block just before the auction ends. No problem—just keep on going after the other properties you are interested in.

Bidding on Properties at Internet Auctions

Making a bid on a property over the Internet is as simple as the click of a mouse. To make a bid on a property, first open your web browser to the auction website. Next, find the auction you are interested in. You can make a bidding folder in your favorite websites and bookmark the actual webpage that holds the auction. Once you're on the bidding page, type in the amount you want to bid. Be sure to confirm your bid, as you cannot take it back.

There are two ways to bid. You can make either a flat bid or an auto bid. A flat bid is one in which you bid an exact bid amount. An auto bid is one in which you indicate the maximum amount you want to bid and the auctioneer will automatically bid for you up to that amount. With an auto bid, the auctioneer will only increase your bid to make you the highest bidder, up to your specified maximum amount. If the bidding exceeds your maximum amount, the auctioneer will not continue to automatically bid for you. You will be outbid unless you manually make a higher offer.

For example, suppose that in an auction with $100 increments the opening bid on a property is $100. You place a bid for a maximum amount of $700, with the next highest increment to put you to the highest bid, but not more than $700. If you're the first bidder, your bid will be $100. If someone else bids $200, the computer will automatically increase your bid to $300. If someone later bids $500, your bid will automatically increase to $600. However, if someone bids $700, your automatic bidding will stop, because you did not authorize it to go to $800.

During the auction, you will have to periodically check on your bids. Throughout the auction, other people will be bidding on the same property. You will need to see if you are the high bidder or whether someone else has become the high bidder. To check if there are any higher bids, you may have to hit "refresh" on your web browser.

Bidding Strategies

Now, knowing that you can auto bid, you can see what someone else's maximum bid amount is. If you place a flat bid on a property and suddenly you are not the highest bidder, then someone has auto bidding in place. You can place consecutive flat bids higher and higher until their maximum auto bid is reached.

One strategy is to make a bid that greatly increases the bid, say from $1,000 to $3,000. This is a big jump in price as compared to going from $1,000 to $1,100. A big jump in a bid will scare off a lot of bidders in an Internet auction. It gives the message that you are serious about buying the property and want to get rid of the less serious buyers. It also eliminates bidders who don't have the money to bid that high.

The Hour Before the End of the Auction

Make sure you are aware of the time zone in which the auction is conducted. You could end up looking at a property whose auction ends at 5 p.m. Pacific time, when it actually ended three hours ago, Eastern time.

Most of the action will be in the last minutes of the auction. You will see many increases right before the property's expiration. Log on to the website at least half an hour before the auction's expiration. This will ensure that you can get on the website. A lot of people who are interested in the same property will use up a lot of site's traffic, which can slow down or even crash a website.

Bidding at the last minute is called snipping. With snipping, you wait until the last minute to bid on the property. This will save you a lot of time checking bids. With this strategy, however, you risk someone else having a maximum bid amount that is higher than your maximum bid. You also can put in a maximum bid amount at the last minute. I recommend the snipping strategy.

Extended Time

At a live auction, the bidding continues until the highest bid has been offered. Internet auctions do the same thing with extended time. Although there is a deadline by which you must submit a bid, the bidding will continue past that deadline, as long as there are competing bidders.

The Internet auctioneer will extend the deadline to place a bid for an additional five minutes after a higher bid is placed. This allows additional time for any competing bidders to place even higher bids. This extension of time will go on indefinitely until there are no more higher bids.

What Happens if the Highest Bidder Does Not Complete the Purchase?

In an Internet auction, properties are not put back up for sale because someone has not paid for the property. If some joker has bid on a property and doesn't end up paying for it, the property will not be auctioned off again in the current auction but may be in the next one. So keep your bidding information in a safe place. If the property comes up again in the next auction, you can use the same research.

Chapter 9

Open the Envelope, Please: Sealed Bid Auctions

Chapter Overview

In this chapter, you will learn the following:

1. What are sealed bid tax sale auctions?
2. How to bid at a tax sale auction
3. Strategies for sealed bid tax sale auctions

Introduction

Sealed bid auctions are the least used auction method. This type of auction does not promote aggressive competitive bidding as do live and Internet auctions. In live and Internet auctions, you can see the property being bid up, and many people get caught up in that, which typically results in higher final sale prices.

About Sealed Bid Auctions

In a sealed bid auction, bidders submit their bids to the county. This is not competitive bidding. There is no way of knowing how much other bidders are bidding. You won't even know how many bids are submitted, and you can only submit one bid per property. Usually, the county reserves the right to review and accept or reject any bid.

How to Bid

The tax collector will have bid sheets. Fill out your bid sheet with your personal information, the property you want to bid on, and the amount you want to bid.

Sometimes the bid sheet allows you to bid up to a certain amount. You will be the high bidder if no one overbids you. In this type of auction, the purchase price will be the highest amount that makes you the high bidder.

In this type of auction, put your best foot forward and hope no one overbids you. This is a "wait and see what you get" process.

Be Aware of the Deadline

The last thing you want to do in a sealed bid auction is to miss the cut-off time. There will be a deadline by which you must submit your bid, and no more bids will be accepted after that time. So make sure you get your bid in on time.

Bidding Strategies

There are basically two strategies to bidding at sealed bid auctions. The first is to bid the highest amount that you are willing to offer for a particular property or properties. The second strategy is the low-ball shotgun approach.

The first strategy involves calculating the maximum amount you are willing to pay for the property and bidding that amount. Give what you feel is a fair tax sale auction price for the property but not more. You almost have to close your eyes and hope for the best. All you can do is bid the most that you are willing to bid. You are more likely to be the winning bidder with this strategy.

The second strategy is to bid on a lot of properties but to offer low amounts. With this strategy you probably will not win all of your bids, if any. But the bids that you do win will be well worth the effort.

PART III
Little Known Tips and Tricks for After the Tax Sale Auction

Chapter 10

The 19th Hole: What to Do After the Auction

Chapter Overview

In this chapter, you will learn the following:

1. How to pay for the property after the tax sale auction
2. When do you own the property?
3. How to get insurance for the property
4. The importance of transferring utilities to the property
5. Why you should contact the homeowners association

Introduction

Congratulations! You survived your first tax sale. You started out by finding and researching properties. Then you picked some properties you were interested in. You participated in the tax sale auction, and you actually came out on top as the successful bidder. You've gone a lot farther than most people. You deserve to celebrate!

Your job, however, is not done yet. I know it's been a long process, but there are a few more things you need to do. Stick with it. You have to think of the marathon runner. When the finish line is in sight, the professional runner does not slow down. A good runner finishes strong and picks up the pace at the end. Now that you have been the successful bidder at a tax sale, remember to finish strong.

Pay for the Property

If you paid for your property in full at the time of the auction, you can skip this section since it does not apply to you. However, if you only paid a deposit at the tax sale, and not the full purchase price, read on.

Most winning bidders at a tax sale place a deposit on the property. A common deposit amount is $5,000. The county requires that you pay off the balance of the purchase price within a short period of time (usually one week). For example, say your winning bid on a property is $12,000 and you put down a $5,000 deposit. You must pay the remaining $7,000 within a week to complete your purchase. If you do not pay the full $7,000 within a week, you will not be able to purchase the property and you will lose your $5,000 deposit.

I cannot reiterate enough the importance of paying the full purchase price before the deadline. The worst thing you could do is to forget to pay the rest of the bid price. All of your hard work will go to waste and you will lose your deposit. Remember, time is not on your side. The county has a deadline for you to pay the remainder of the purchase price. DO NOT LET THE DEADLINE PASS WITHOUT PAYING THE FULL PURCHASE PRICE. Any deposit you made will be lost and there are no refunds.

When you go to the tax collector's office to pay off the purchase price, get a receipt for any funds that you pay.

If you do not pay the full balance, the sale will be terminated since it is not complete. When the sale is not complete, the county will not deed the property to you, you will forfeit your deposit, and your deposit money will not be refunded to you.

When Do You Own the Property?

You do not own the property immediately after the tax sale. If you are the successful bidder at the tax sale and you pay for the property in full, you do not own the property until the county <u>records</u> the tax sale deed. You will be the owner from the day of recording of the tax sale deed. Check with the county tax collector and the county recorder to see whether the tax sale deed has been recorded.

Until the date of recording, you can't do anything with the property because you don't own it. It usually takes the county several weeks to record the tax sale deed. After recording, you will receive the tax deed in the mail within a couple weeks.

Get Fire Insurance

If the property is anything but vacant land, you will want to insure it. The minimum type of insurance to get is fire insurance. Fire insurance will pay you to replace the improvements on the property in case the property is partially or wholly destroyed by fire.

To be eligible to purchase insurance, you must have an insurable interest. The risk of loss passes at the time of the tax sale. So you will want to get fire insurance right away. As soon as you are the successful bidder and make a deposit or pay for the property, you have an insurable interest in it.

Ask your insurance agent to get fire insurance for the property. Insure the property in an amount equal to at least 80 to 90% of its fair market value (not what you paid for it). This is required by the co-insurance clause of your insurance policy. The reason for this is that an insurance company can partially deny your claim if you don't get enough insurance. They will penalize you for being underinsured by denying your claim.

For example, let's say your property is worth $100,000, but you only get insurance coverage for $70,000. A fire damages the property for a loss of $50,000. This is less than your insurance coverage of $70,000 and is also less than the full value of the property of $100,000. The insurance company can say you violated the co-insurance clause and are underinsured. In such a case, instead of paying you $50,000 (the amount of your loss) it will only pay you $35,000 (70% of $50,000).

Other Types of Insurance

There are many other types of insurance besides fire insurance. I mention some of them here to familiarize you with them. Discuss with your insurance agent which types of insurance and which policy limits are best for you and your property. Here is a list of the different types of insurance:

- Homeowner's insurance
- Earthquake insurance
- Flood insurance
- General liability insurance
- Course of construction insurance
- Terrorist insurance

Of these different types of insurance, the most useful is general liability insurance. This will protect you against lawsuits from accidents on the property, such as a "slip and falls."

For vacant land, there are no improvements (buildings and structures) to insure. The only type of insurance to get is general liability insurance. But very few people ever get it for raw land. Land is not insurable against loss—only improvements are.

Transfer the Utilities

Now that you own the property, you will need to put the utilities in your name. With vacant land, however, you won't have any utilities. The most common types of utilities are the following:

- Electricity
- Gas
- Water
- Trash service
- Cable television

Some utilities come with shares. This is often true of mutual water companies. Mutual water companies are water companies that are owned by the owners of the properties served by the water company. Each property must have one or more water company shares of stock. If this is true in your area, have the water company transfer the ownership of the shares into your name.

Notify the Homeowners Association

Condominiums, planned urban developments (PUDs), and time-shares have some type of homeowners association. The homeowners association is in charge of the common areas and exterior of the properties. Sometimes the development will have a swimming pool, spa, meeting room, or workout room. The homeowners association maintains these facilities as well as the landscaping and the exterior of the units.

If you buy a condo, PUD or time-share, you will have to notify the homeowners association of your new ownership of the property. There also will be monthly dues to pay.

Chapter 11

Cleaning House: What to Do With the Tenants

Chapter Overview

In this chapter, you will learn the following:

1. What to do about existing tenants
2. How to serve various notices to the tenants
3. What to do about the previous owner
4. How to get the tenants out sooner

Introduction

Not all properties will have tenants occupying them. For those that do have tenants, you'll need to meet them and inform them where to send their rent. You also will have some decisions to make as to whether or not to keep them.

Ideally, you should go in person to the property and meet whoever is occupying the property. The occupant may either be a tenant or the previous owner of the property. At the same time, you should inspect the condition of the property. A checklist to inspect the property is included in Appendix A.

A Tenant Occupies the Property

If a tenant occupies the property, you may be met with a great deal of confusion and distrust when you initially inform them that you are the new owner of the property from the tax sale. Often, the tenants have no idea that the property has been sold.

Determine which type of tenancy the existing tenants have. They will either have a month-to-month tenancy or a lease. You can ask the tenant which type of tenancy they have and then use a tenant estoppel certificate to determine the terms of the tenancy with the tenant. Once a tenant signs a tenant estoppel certificate, he cannot later say that the terms of the rental are any different from what he stated in the tenant estoppel certificate. An example of a tenant estoppel certificate is in Appendix B.

After meeting with the tenant in person, send him a letter explaining that you are the new owner of the property. In the letter, explain where to send the rent. An example of an initial letter to the tenant is in Appendix C.

Terminating the Tenancy

It does not matter whether the tenant has a month-to-month tenancy or has a lease that is not yet expired, the tax sale will terminate the tenancy. You also can choose to terminate the tenancy at any time with the proper written notice. An oral notice to move is not sufficient. You must give a 30-day written notice. An example of a 30-day notice is in Appendix D. However, if you accept rent from the tenant, the tenancy will continue on a month-to-month tenancy. You can collect the rent from the tenant from the day that your tax deed is recorded.

What if the Tenant Does Not Pay the Rent?

You have a right to collect the rent. If the tenant does not pay rent, give him a three-day notice, an example of which is in Appendix E.

Calculating the three-day period is tricky. You must not count the day of serving the notice, but you count ever other calendar day. For example, if you serve the tenant on a Monday, you count Tuesday as the first day. The three-day period expires on Thursday. The earliest that you can file the unlawful detainer action in court is Friday. The least favorable day for a landlord to serve a three-day notice is Tuesday. The earliest day you can file the unlawful eviction is Monday, as long as it's not a holiday. That's a full week to end your three-day notice period!

Once the three-day period has expired, start the unlawful detainer action in court. For this, get an experienced eviction attorney.

The Previous Owner Resides in the Property

If the previous owner occupies the property, he probably will not be happy that you now own the property from the tax sale. Avoid any hostilities. Do not get into any yelling matches. Keep it cordial, because you will need to discuss important issues with the previous owner.

I suggest that you ask the previous owner to move from the property as soon as possible. There are several reasons for this:

1. The previous owner may be angry and vindictive enough to be destructive to the property.

2. The previous owner will always have animosity toward you.

3. You can get a better tenant that you screen yourself.

If the person occupying the property is the previous owner, you do not have to give any written notice. The owner of the property is not a tenant with tenancy rights. The law calls the previous owner a tenant at sufferance (which is a big legal term meaning he has no right to possession) and can be evicted immediately by an unlawful detainer. No notice is required to start an unlawful detainer against the previous owner of the property.

But wait a minute. You mean the owner of the property is sitting in the property, sweating bullets because you bought it out from under him at the tax sale and you can't think of a way to use this to your advantage? We'll talk about this some more when we discuss clearing title.

Cash for Keys

Just as there is more than one way to skin a cat, there is more than one way to get a tenant to move. My favorite method is to offer money to the tenant in exchange for moving sooner. I call it "cash for keys."

Typically, I offer the tenant $400 if he will move out of the property by the end of the current month (as long as there is at least a week left in the month). You can offer more or less if you want. I explain that the tenant will get the $400 only after he has removed all of his belongings from the premises and has left the premises in a broom-swept clean condition. I also explain that if the tenant does not move out by that date, he will not get any money and I will start the eviction action.

DO NOT RELY ON AN ORAL AGREEMENT. Always get the agreement in writing. When you agree to pay the tenant to move out, have him sign a letter of intent to vacate. If he fails to move out, this will allow you to start an eviction action without any further notices. An example of a letter of intent to vacant is in Appendix F.

This is a win-win situation. Here are the benefits to the tenant:

1. The tenant gets money he wouldn't get otherwise.

2. The tenant avoids an eviction on his credit report, which could prevent him from renting elsewhere.

3. The tenant avoids a money judgment of rent, fees, and interest.

4. The tenant avoids the cost and time of fighting an eviction action

Here are the benefits to you:

1. You get the property clean and empty.

2. You get the property vacant sooner than with an eviction action.

3. You avoid the lost rents you would incur during the eviction action.

4. You avoid a lot of headache.

The reason I offer $400 is because this is approximately the cost of an eviction action. I figure I can either pay an eviction attorney to move the tenant out in a couple months or pay the tenant to move out sooner.

Giving cash for keys is completely legal. An eviction action is a civil lawsuit about money and possession of the property. Every lawsuit can be settled by the parties before or during litigation (in fact, the courts encourage it). The tenant moves out, and then you pay him a cash settlement.

It's all perfectly legal. It will be cheaper, faster, and less hassle for you to settle the case by giving the tenant cash for his keys.

The Tenant's Security Deposit

What about the tenant's security deposit? Well, you take the property at the tax sale with all its benefits and burdens. If the tenant moves out, you must pay back the security deposit, even though you did not collect the security deposit from the previous owner. Ask the tenant to produce the receipt from the previous owner to prove the amount of the security deposit.

You still can make the usual deductions from the security deposit, such as a cleaning fee and the cost of damage beyond normal wear and tear to the dwelling. In an eviction action, the tenant often forfeits the security deposit, meaning you don't have to pay it back.

Chapter 12

Knowledge Is Power: Know the Title Issues

Chapter Overview

In this chapter, you will learn the following:

1. How to pay off liens that were not removed at the tax sale
2. How to know what kind of title you get at the tax sale
3. The previous owner's rights in the property

Introduction

Given the inherent nature of tax sales, you take the property without any title insurance. Now that you purchased a property at a tax sale, you will have to clear the title. There are several methods of doing this.

Pay off Any Remaining Liens

There are some, but not many, liens that are not wiped out by a tax sale. In any case, these liens do not amount to more than a few hundred dollars at most.

You can find the liens through your research of the property. Contact the lien holders and pay off these liens. Make sure to get a receipt.

Once you pay off the lien, the lien holder should issue you a lien release. Record the lien release immediately with the county recorder. This will release the lien from the title of the property.

The following are types of liens you may have to pay off:

1. Special assessment installments due after the sale or which were not included in the amount fixed for presale redemption of the property.

2. Liens for taxes levied by any agency that has not consented to the sale. Different taxing authorities, such as a water district, school district, or redevelopment agency have rights to property taxes.

Framing the Title Problem

First let's gain an understanding of why there might be a problem with the title to the property. The problem with tax sales is the previous owner's right to sue the county for an improper tax sale. If the previous owner sues the county, it puts a cloud on title. It is uncertain who will ultimately end up with the property until a one-year period is up. If a lawsuit is filed during this one-year period, you will have to wait even longer until the lawsuit is completely resolved, including appeals.

The problem is the uncertainty and risk. You cannot get a title policy on the property. This means you cannot transfer the property or get a trust deed against the property. The money you paid for the property is at risk.

This is something you'll want to clear up as soon as possible. Fortunately, you have many ways to do this. I'll show you how later in this book.

What Kind of Title Do You Get?

In a nutshell, when you purchase a tax sale property you get the best kind of title possible. When you get a tax sale deed, you receive a new and complete title under an independent grant directly from the state or county. You get the property free and clear of all private monetary liens. These private monetary liens include all deeds of trust (mortgages), mechanic's liens, judgment liens, state tax liens, and federal tax liens (if the Internal Revenue Service is properly notified), etc.

At the tax sale, you are not getting title from the previous owner, with all its potential flaws. You are getting a superior title at the tax sale. In fact, you often get a better title than the previous owner had. It is free from any unrecorded deeds or other defects in title.

Previous Owner's Right to Sue the County

Contrary to popular belief, the previous owner of the property does <u>not</u> have the right to redeem the property from the purchaser at a tax sale. The previous owner's right to redeem the property ends the business day before the tax sale. That's why tax sales often begin on a Monday. The last business day for the defaulting owner to pay the back taxes is the previous Friday.

As mentioned, the previous owner has the right to sue the county for conducting the sale improperly. This is a lawsuit about due process. Due process requires 1) notice and 2) an opportunity to be heard. The county always provides an opportunity to be heard, so these lawsuits hinge on the notice that was given to the owner.

If the notice was not properly given, the previous owner's due process rights were violated and the sale was improper. In such a (rare) case, the county must compensate the owner, either through payment of the fair market value of the property or through forcing the purchaser to return the property to the previous owner. The purchaser at the tax sale is reimbursed for the purchase price and all expenses of the sale.

If the notice was properly given, the previous owner was given due process. Then the tax sale was properly conducted and the previous owner is out of luck. This concept is important, as we will later discuss this again on how to clear title.

I want to note that although the lawsuit is against the county, the purchaser will most likely be a party to the lawsuit. This is to prevent the purchaser from transferring the property, encumbering the property, or committing waste. It also gives the court jurisdiction over the purchaser to order him to transfer the property back to the previous owner. In this vein, there will be a lis pendens against the title to the property, which will cloud title.

Chapter 13

Smoothing Out the Wrinkles: Clearing title

Chapter Overview

In this chapter, you will learn the following:

1. How to clear title
2. How to settle with a quitclaim deed
3. How to get the title company's help
4. Suing to clear title
5. Waiting a year to clear title

Introduction

Now we get to the good stuff. You won't see this information anywhere else. With these solutions, you won't have to wait a year to do what you want with the property. I've presented these solutions in the ways I think are best to resolve the problems. Try them in the order in which they are presented.

Settle With a Quitclaim Deed

The best way to clear title is by settling with the previous owner(s) by having them sign a settlement agreement and a quitclaim deed. Examples of each are respectively shown in Appendix G and Appendix H. This will relinquish all rights the previous owners had in the property to you.

You can do this as a settlement to a lawsuit. If the previous owner does not release his rights in the property, you will have to sue him and have the court resolve the issue. Few people who just lost a property in a tax sale want the additional headache of fighting a lawsuit.

Offer the previous owner money to settle. This will sweeten the pot. Forget the principle of the matter. Lawsuits are about money. If you can get the person to settle with a quitclaim deed, then you've already won. Pay for the notary fees, which are about $10 per signature. Pay for the recording fees, which are less than $20. Offer to help the previous owner get his excess proceeds of the tax sale.

If the previous owner is a corporation, you must have an authorized officer of the corporation sign the quitclaim deed. If the previous owner is a limited liability company, you must either have an authorized member or manager sign. If the previous owner is a trust, you must have the trustees sign. If the previous owner is a partnership, you must have the general partner or all partners sign.

Remember that all of the co-owners of the property must settle, including their spouses. In community property states, a property owned by one spouse can be claimed by the other spouse as community property. Because of this, you must have both spouses sign the quitclaim deed, even if only one spouse is on title. If someone else owns the property in joint tenancy or as a tenant in common, all of the previous owners must sign the quitclaim deed.

If only some of the owners sign the quitclaim deed, the others still have a right to sue. In such a case, a cloud on title still exists. Don't settle for this. This method is all signatures or nothing.

Once you have a signed settlement agreement and notarized quitclaim deed, record them. Show the quitclaim deed to your title company. This will clear the title.

If you are successful in having the previous owners sign a settlement agreement and a quitclaim deed, it is a guaranteed win. This is a relatively low-cost method. You've got nothing to lose by offering this settlement. You will even look better in the court's mind by offering a settlement instead of litigation. This method offers quick results and you'll know immediately if you are successful.

Settling With the Previous Owner:
Pros:
1. This method is fast.
2. This method is relatively cheap.
Con:
1. Many people are not comfortable dealing with the previous owner.

Title Insurance Company

Here's where your relationship with your title company will pay off. Let your title rep know in advance what you plan to do and how their services will help.

It goes something like this. You have your title insurance company, or an affiliated company, research the previous owner's rights in the case. They basically will research the notice requirements and whether they have been fulfilled by the county. This is all about notice to the previous owner. If everything checks out okay, you will get a guarantee of clear title.

You can expect to pay a fee of between $750 and $1,250. This is inexpensive compared to the cost of litigation. Besides this research fee, you will have to get a title policy, the cost of which is based on your purchase price of the property.

Once the notice is researched and you get title insurance on the property, you have cleared title. Now you can freely transfer the property and get a trust deed.

This method is non-confrontational and is the middle of the road as far as costs are concerned. It also offers relatively quick results.

Title Company Services:
Pros:
1. It is an easy solution.
2. It does not require any confrontation with the previous owner.
Cons:
1. It may not be available in your area.
2. It is of modest cost.

Sue His Pants Off

You can file a lawsuit asking the court to determine all interests in the property. Only do this after trying to settle the case by quitclaim deed.

The name of the lawsuit is a quiet title action. You sue anyone and everyone who has an actual or potential interest in the property. You sue the previous owners, their spouses, trust deed holders, lien holders, and easement holders.

Just because you sue, it doesn't mean the lawsuit will go all the way to trial. Filing a lawsuit may induce the previous owner to settle. Many cases are settled by the parties during litigation, often when the chances of winning are uncertain or slim.

Suing the Previous Owner:
    Pros:
        1. You have a deed on certain title declared by the court.
        2. There is no doubt as to the ownership of the property.
    Cons:
        1. This is the most expensive method.
        2. This is the most confrontational method.
        3. This method is time consuming.

Wait One Year

This is the passive approach. You simply wait until the statute of limitations is over. If the previous owner does not file a lawsuit, then you have cleared the cloud on title. You will be able to get title insurance, transfer the property, and get a trust deed.

This method is one of the cheapest. You can use the income from the property to pay the property's bills. However, you will have to give back the excess income over the expenses of the property.

    Wait It Out:
        Pro:
            1. This method is the least expensive
        Cons:
            1. This method takes a lot of time
            2. This is the most passive method

Transfer the Property Anyway

There is risk to transferring the property within the first year without first having performed one of the above title-clearing methods.

An owner's policy of title, called an ALTA policy (American Land Title Association), protects the transferor or property against title defects. It also gives the transferee a recovery method to correct such title defects. The transfer will be done without title insurance. Without title insurance, the transferor is responsible to the transferee.

If you're going to transfer the property anyway, it is best to disclose all facts. You must disclose that you purchased the property at a county tax sale. You must disclose that the previous owner has a right to sue the county for an improper sale for one year from the sale date. You must disclose that because of the previous owner's rights, you cannot give marketable title to the property. You must disclose that if such a lawsuit is filed, and if it is successful, the previous owner may be entitled to get the property back.

Transfer the Property Anyway
    Pros:
        1. Fast results
        2. No confrontation with previous owner
    Cons:
        1. Very risky transfer
        2. You open yourself to liability.

Appendix A

Assessor's Parcel Map Examples

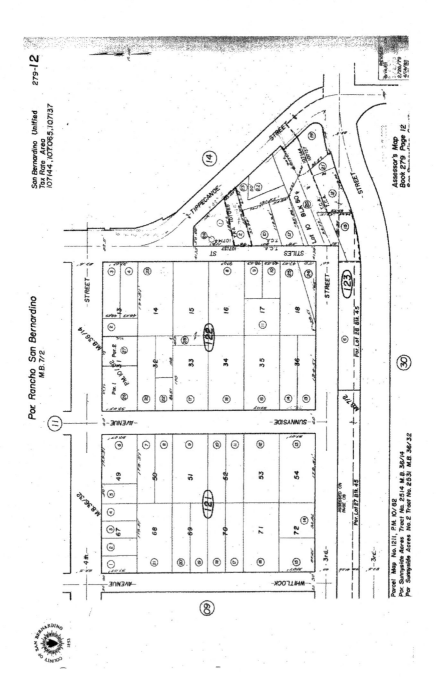

Por. Rancho San Bernardino
M.B. 7/2

San Bernardino Unified
Tax Rate Area
107144, 107065, 107137

279-12

Assessor's Map
Book 279 Page 12

Parcel Map No. 1211, P.M. 10/62
Por. Sunnyside Acres Tract No. 2514 M.B. 36/14
Por. Sunnyside Acres No. 2 Tract No. 2531 M.B. 36/32

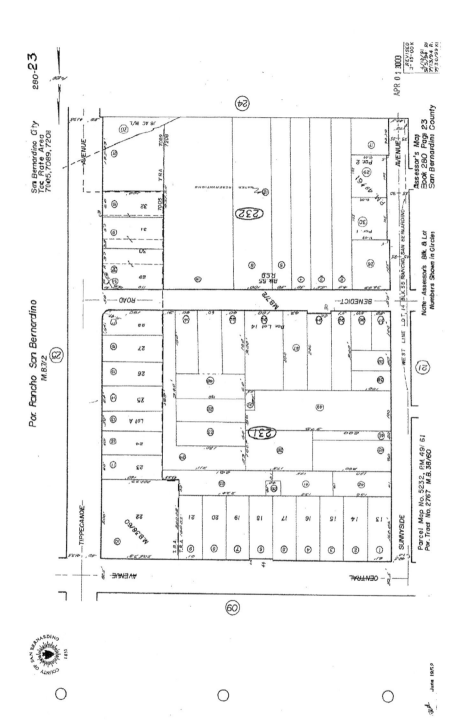

280-23

San Bernardino City
Tax Rate Area
7005,7089,7208

Por. Rancho San Bernardino
M.B.7/2

Assessor's Map
Book 280 Page 23
San Bernardino County

Note—Assessor's Blk. & Lot
Numbers Shown in Circles

Parcel Map No. 5232, P.M. 49/61
Por. Tract No. 2767 M.B. 38/60

APR 0 1 1000

June 1959

97

Appendix B

Letter to the Owner of the Property

Your name
Address
City, State, Zip
Phone

Owner's Name
Address
City, State, Zip

Date

Dear Mr(s). _____:

I am a neighbor of yours. I live at (address). I'm a bit concerned about you because I learned you may be in a bit of a bind. I discovered that your property is up for auction at the _____ County tax sale. I'm here to help.

I'm in the market to buy property right now and I really like your property. I could help you save your property and put cash in your pocket. I'll do it quickly and confidentially.

Time is ticking, so please call me at (____) _____. I know if we put our heads together, we can come up with something to get you out of your jam. Thanks a lot.

Best regards,

_____

Appendix C

Tax Sale Bid Sheet

Tax Sale Bid Sheet

Property Information

Property address _____

Legal description _____

County _____ Assessor's parcel number _____

Fair market value of property _____

Current use of property _____ Zoning _____

Comments _____

Auction Information

Auction date(s) _____ Auction start time _____

Auction end time _____

Auction address (live auctions) _____

For Internet auctions:

    Auction website _____

    My email address _____

    Username _____ Password _____

Registration Information

Registration deadline _____ Registered ☐ Yes ☐ No

Registration name _____

Deposit amount required _____ Deposit paid: ☐ Yes ☐ No

Bidding information

Auction item number _____

Opening bid _____ Bidding increments _____

Maximum I will pay for this property _____

Appendix D

Property Condition Checklist

General Property Information

Property address: _____

A.P.N.: _____ Tax Sale Auction #_____

Property type: ☐ Single family residence ☐ Condo ☐ PUD
☐ Time-share ☐ Vacant Land ☐ Commercial ☐ Industrial

Bed: _____ Bath: _____ Sq. Ft.: _____ Year built: _____

Lot size: _____ Occupancy: ☐ Occupied ☐ Vacant

Notes: _____

Exterior Condition

Exterior condition: _____ Neighborhood condition: _____

Roof type: ☐ Composition Shingle ☐ Tile ☐ Wood shake

Roof condition: _____ Roof age: _____ years

Ext. finish: ☐ Stucco ☐ Wood/Alum. siding ☐ Brick ☐ Block

Garage: ☐ Attached ☐ Detached # of cars _____ ☐ Carport

Is the lot level: ☐ Yes ☐ No explain: _____

Apparent easements on the property: _____

Utilities in street: ☐ Elec. ☐ Water ☐ Sewer ☐ Gas ☐ Phone

Off-site improve.: ☐ Asphalt ☐ Curb/gutter ☐ Sidewalk ☐
Street light ☐ Fire hydrant

☐ Patio ☐ Porch ☐ Deck ☐ Pool ☐ Spa ☐ Gazebo ☐ Shed

Landscaping: ☐ Grass ☐ Shrubs ☐ Trees ☐ Sprinklers

Fencing: ☐ Chain link ☐ Wrought iron ☐ Block ☐ Wood

View: _____

Notes: _____

Interior Condition

Kitchen: ☐ Refrig ☐ Stove/oven ☐ Garbage Disp.
☐ Dishwasher ☐ Fan/hood ☐ Microwave

Kit. Countertops: ☐ Formica ☐ Tile ☐ Granite ☐ Other _____

Cond. of walls: _____ Water-damaged ceilings: ☐ Yes ☐ No

☐ Fireplace ☐ Washer/dryer hookups

HVAC: ☐ Central air ☐ Central heat ☐ Evaporative cooler ☐
Wall/floor furnace

Floors: ☐ Carpet ☐ Tile ☐ Linoleum ☐ Hard wood

Notes: _____

Appendix E

Tenant Estoppel Certificate

TENANT ESTOPPEL CERTIFICATE

Tenant's Name(s): _____

Property Address: _____

To Whom It May Concern:

1. The undersigned is the Tenant of the above property under the following terms:

    (□ If checked) A copy of the Rental Agreement/Lease is attached hereto.

    □ Tenancy is on a month-to-month basis

    □ Tenancy is a lease with lease expiration on _____

    Date of the Rental Agreement/Lease: _____

    Name of the original Landlord:

    _____

    Name of the current Landlord (if different):

    _____

    Name of the original Tenant (if different):

    _____

    Current monthly rent: $_____, paid through: _____

    Security Deposit: $_____

    The following appliances belonging to tenant: □ Refrig □ Stove/oven □ Dishwasher □ Microwave □ Washer □ Dryer □ Evaporative Cooler

    There are _____ adults and _____ children esiding at the Property

2. Tenant acknowledges that there are no verbal or other written agreements between Landlord and Tenant with respect to the Property, except as stated below:

_____

_____

_____

3. Tenant has not assigned or sublet his/her/their tenancy in the Property.

4. Tenant has not received any free rent, partial rent, or concessions of any kind, except as follows:

_____

_____

_____

5. The Landlord is not in breach of any term of the Rental Agreement/Lease. Tenant has no defenses, offsets or counterclaims to the payment of rent under the Rental Agreement/Lease.

6. Tenant declares that (A) he/she/they are not in default of the performance of any obligations under the Rental Agreement/Lease; (B) has not breached the Rental Agreement/Lease in any way; and (C) has not received any notices under the Rental Agreement/Lease, which has not been cured.

7. All notices to the Tenant can be sent to the Property.

8. Tenant acknowledges that a buyer may rely on the statements made by Tenant in this Certificate.

I HAVE READ AND UNDERSTAND THE ABOVE AND I AGREE TO ABIDE BY ITS TERMS AND CONDITIONS.

_____   _____
Tenant's Signature   Date

_____   _____
Tenant's Signature   Date

Appendix F

Initial Letter to Tenant

Tenant's Name
Address
City, State Zip

Date

RE: Tenancy at [address of property]

Dear Mr(s). [tenant's name]:

You are hereby notified that I am the new owner of the above referenced property as of [date of recording].

The contact information and address for all notices shall be the following:

> Your name
> Your address
> Your city, state, zip
> Your phone number

Please make all rent checks payable to [name]. Your monthly rent in the amount of [amount] is due on the first day of each month and is late by the [date] of each month. A late fee of [amount] shall be due on any late payments.

If any of these terms differ from the existing terms of your tenancy, please accept this letter as a written modification of the terms of your tenancy.

If you have any questions, please call me at [phone number]. Thank you for your cooperation.

Best regards,

[your name, title]

Appendix G

30-Day Notice

30-DAY NOTICE
TO TERMINATE TENANCY

TO: [tenant's name(s)]

      TAKE NOTICE that your month-to-month tenancy of the hereinafter described premises is hereby terminated as of the thirty (30) days after the service of this NOTICE upon you. YOU ARE HEREBY required to quit and surrender possession thereof to the undersigned on or before the date thirty (30) days after service of this NOTICE upon you.

      The premises of which you are required to surrender possession are:

        [property address]
        [property city, state, zip]

THIS IS INTENDED AS A THIRTY (30) DAY LEGAL NOTICE
FOR THE PURPOSE OF TERMINATING YOUR TENANCY

[your name]
[your address]
[your phone number]
[your business hours (example: Mon. thru Fri., 9 a.m. to 5 p.m.)]

Dated: _____   _____
                                     [your name]

PROOF OF SERVICE – 30-DAY NOTICE TO QUIT

I, THE UNDERSIGNED, declare:
1. I am a citizen of the United States and a resident of the County of _____ I am, and at all times herein mentioned, was over the age of eighteen years. My business address is [business address].
2. I served the within Thirty-Day Notice to Quit in the manner indicated below:
( ) By delivering a copy to the tenant personally on _____ (date).
( ) The tenant being absent from his home or usual place of business, by leaving a copy with some person of suitable age and discretion on _____ and thereafter sending a copy through the mail addressed to the tenant at his place of business on _____ (date).
( ) If such place of business cannot be ascertained, or a person of suitable age or discretion there cannot be found, then by affixing a copy in a conspicuous place on the property on _____ (date) and also delivering a copy to a person there residing, if such person can be found; and thereafter sending a copy through the mail addressed to the tenant at the place where the property is situated on _____.
The property is located at _____
in the City of _____, State of _____.
I declare under penalty of perjury that the foregoing is true and correct and that this declaration was executed at the City of _____, State of _____, on _____.

Signature: _____
              Name: [your printed name]

113

Appendix H

Three-Day Notice

THREE-DAY NOTICE TO
PAY RENT OR MOVE OUT

[your name, Plaintiff]   ("Owner")
                VS.
[tenant's name(s)], Defendant(s)   ("Resident(s)")

TO [tenant's name(s)], Resident(s) AND ALL OTHERS IN POSSESSION. PLEASE TAKE NOTICE that you are justly indebted to the Owner of the herein described premises; and notice is hereby given that pursuant to the lease and/or rental agreement there is now due, unpaid and delinquent rent in the total sum of [amount] DOLLARS ($_____).
The total amount owing represents rent due for the following period(s): $_____ Due from [date] through [date] WITHIN THREE (3) DAYS after service on you of this notice, you are hereby required to pay the amount of the above stated rent in full OR quit the subject premises, move out, and deliver up possession to the Owner.
The premises herein referred to which are now held and/or occupied by you are:
        [property address]
        IN THE COUNTY OF _____ , STATE OF _____
PLEASE TAKE FURTHER NOTICE that unless you pay the rent in full OR vacate the premises WITHIN THREE (3) DAYS, the undersigned does hereby elect to declare a forfeiture of the subject lease and/or rental agreement and will institute legal proceedings for an unlawful detainer against you to recover possession of the premises plus court costs, attorney fees, and THREE TIMES THE AMOUNT OF RENT AND DAMAGES due as provided by State law.
        [your address]
        [your phone number]
        [your business hours (Mon. thru Fri., 9 a.m. to 5 p.m.)]
Dated: _____   _____
                                        [your name]

PROOF OF SERVICE – 3-DAY NOTICE TO PAY RENT OR MOVE OUT

I, THE UNDERSIGNED, declare:
1. I am a citizen of the United States and a resident of the County of _____ I am, and at all times herein mentioned, was over the age of eighteen years. My business address is [business address].
2. I served the within Three-Day Notice to Pay Rent or Move Out in the manner indicated below:
( ) By delivering a copy to the tenant personally on _____ (date).
( ) The tenant being absent from his home or usual place of business, by leaving a copy with some person of suitable age and discretion on _____ and thereafter sending a copy through the mail addressed to the tenant at his place of business on _____ (date).
( ) If such place of business cannot be ascertained, or a person of suitable age or discretion there cannot be found, then by affixing a copy in a conspicuous place on the property on _____ (date) and also delivering a copy to a person there residing, if such person can be found; and thereafter sending a copy through the mail addressed to the tenant at the place where the property is situated on _____.

The property is located at _____
in the City of _____, State of _____.
I declare under penalty of perjury that the foregoing is true and correct and that this declaration was executed at the City of _____, State of _____, on _____.

Signature: _____
Name: [your printed name]

117

Appendix I

Tenant's Intent to Vacate

NOTICE OF INTENT TO VACATE

Date: _____

Please be advised that the undersigned intends to vacate those premises known as:

        [property address]
        [property city, state, zip]
        IN THE COUNTY OF _____, STATE OF ____

In conformance with the Civil Code of the State of _____ and/or the rental agreement which states that a written notice of sixty (60) days in advance of a termination must be given, I intend to move on _____.

I am fully aware that the rent in the amount of _____ dollars ($_____) is now due and payable this date for the remaining term to and including the date of termination. I have a security deposit of $_____.

The signature(s) below represent(s) all adults now occupying the premises.
Signature: _____
Name: _____
Forwarding Address: _____

[your name]
[your address]
[your city, state, zip]
[your phone]
[your business hours (Hours: Mon. thru Fri., 9 a.m. to 5 p.m.]

Received on: _____   _____
                                  [your name]

Appendix J

Settlement Agreement

SETTLEMENT AGREEMENT

This Agreement made and entered into this ____ day of _____, 20____, by and between _____ ("Transferor"), and _____ ("Transferee") for the following terms and conditions:

Recitals:

Whereas, the subject of this Agreement is that certain real property commonly known as: [address], and whose legal description is: [legal description] (the "Property").

Whereas, Transferor was previously the owner of the Property, until it was sold at the [county name] tax sale on __

Whereas, Transferee was the successful bidder at the [county name] tax sale on _____ and is now the owner of the Property.

Whereas, Transferor has the right under Section 3725 of the California Revenue and Taxation Code to initiate legal proceedings against the county of _____ and/or Transferee.

Therefore, in consideration of the mutual covenants and agreements contained herein, the parties have entered into this Agreement.

Terms and Conditions:

A. Transferor hereby releases any interest that he/she/it/they had in the Property to Transferee.
B. Transferor shall execute a quitclaim deed for the property in favor of Transferee concurrently with this Settlement Agreement.
C. Transferor hereby waives and releases the right to bring legal proceedings under Section 3725 of the California Revenue and Taxation Code against the county of _____ and against Transferee.

D. In consideration for this Agreement, Transferee has paid $_____ to Transferor, receipt of which is hereby acknowledged.
E. This Agreement shall bind Transferor, his/her/its/their heirs successors and assigns.
F. Transferor warrants that he/she/it/they is/are authorized to sign this Agreement.
G. Transferee shall defend, indemnify and hold Transferor, its officers, employees, and agents harmless from and against any and all liability, loss, expense (including reasonable attorneys' fees) or claims for injury or damages arising out of the performance of this Agreement.
H. This Agreement shall be governed by the laws of the State of California.

I HAVE READ AND UNDERSTAND THE TERMS AND CONDITIONS OF THIS AGREEMENT.

Transferor:

Signature: _____ Date: _____

Transferee:

Signature: _____ Date: _____

STATE OF _____
COUNTY OF _____

Subscribed and sworn to (or affirmed) before me on this
_____ day of _____, 20_____ ,
by _____,
proved to me on the basis of satisfactory evidence to be the person(s) who appeared before me.

Signature _____
          (This area for official notarial seal)

123

Appendix K

Quitclaim Deed

RECORDING REQUESTED BY, AND
WHEN RECORDED MAIL TO:

Name

Address

City, State Zip

DOCUMENTARY TRANSFER TAX $_____ SPACE
ABOVE THIS LINE FOR RECORDER'S USE

.....Computed on the consideration or value of property conveyed; OR

.....Computed on the consideration or value less liens or encumbrances
remaining at time of sale

_____
Signature of Declarant or Agent determining tax - Firm Name

QUITCLAIM DEED

FOR A VALUABLE CONSIDERATION, receipt of which is hereby acknowledged,

(Transferor's name and vesting)

do(es) hereby REMISE, RELEASE AND FOREVER QUITCLAIM to

(Transferee's name and vesting)

the real property in the City of _____, County of
_____, State of _____, described as:

(Insert legal description)

Dated:_____   _____
                             Transferor's Name

STATE OF _____
COUNTY OF _____

Subscribed and sworn to (or affirmed) before me on this
_____ day of _____, 20_____ ,
by _____,
proved to me on the basis of satisfactory evidence to be the
person(s) who appeared before me.

Signature _____

CPSIA information can be obtained
at www.ICGtesting.com
Printed in the USA
LVOW01s2337100516
487655LV00037B/799/P